# NUMBER FACTS & JUMPING JACKS

Matching Learning Activities to Learning Readiness

Bob Sornson, PhD, and Laureen Reynolds

Crystal Springs BOOKS
SDE
a division of Staff Development for Educators
Peterborough, New Hampshire

Published by Crystal Springs Books
A division of Staff Development for Educators (SDE)
10 Sharon Road, PO Box 500
Peterborough, NH 03458
1-800-321-0401
www.SDE.com/crystalsprings

© 2011 Early Learning Foundation and Crystal Springs Books
Illustrations © 2011 Crystal Springs Books

Published 2011
Printed in the United States of America
15  14  13  12  11          1  2  3  4  5

ISBN: 978-1-934026-84-7

Library of Congress Cataloging-in-Publication Data
Sornson, Robert.
    Number facts & jumping jacks : matching learning activities to learning readiness / Bob Sornson and Laureen Reynolds.
       p. cm. —(Early learning success)
Includes bibliographical references and index.
ISBN 978-1-934026-84-7
    1. Numeracy—Study and teaching (Early childhood)—Activity programs.
    2. Motor learning—Study and teaching (Early childhood)—Activity programs. I. Reynolds, Laureen, 1969- II. Title. III.
       Title: Number facts and jumping jacks. IV. Series.
QA141.15.S67 2011
372.7—dc22                2010047937

Editor: Sandra J. Taylor
Art Director and Designer: S. Dunholter
Cover Designer: Tamara English, Bill Smith Group
Production Coordinator: Deborah Fredericks
Illustrator: Joyce Rainville

Crystal Springs Books grants the owner of this book the right to photocopy the reproducibles from this book for use in his or her classroom only. No other part of this book may be reproduced in whole or in part, or stored in a retrieval system, or transmitted in any form or by any means, electronic, mechanical, photocopying, recording, or otherwise, without written permission of the publisher.

## Dedication

This book is dedicated to that look in the eyes of a young child, that joy, that state of flow, which comes from immersion in the learning process.

Bob Sornson

# Contents

Introduction .................................................................... 4

Section 1: Numeracy Skills ............................................ 9

Numeracy Skills Profile ................................................ 10

Numeracy Skills Rubric ................................................. 11

Procedures for Assessment of Numeracy Skills ............. 14

Activities for Building Numeracy Skills ......................... 17

Section 2: Gross Motor Skills ........................................ 85

Gross Motor Skills Profile .............................................. 86

Gross Motor Skills Rubric .............................................. 87

Procedures for Assessment of Gross Motor Skills .......... 89

Activities for Building Gross Motor Skills ...................... 91

References ..................................................................... 156

Index ............................................................................. 157

Meeting the Standards ................................................... 160

# Introduction

The goal of this book is to ensure that every child is given the opportunity to build the solid foundation of essential skills that is needed for lifelong learning success. Focusing on two areas of development—numeracy and gross motor skills—*Number Facts & Jumping Jacks* provides tools for determining which skills a child has or has not yet developed. In addition, it provides more than 300 activities to help you devise an instructional plan that fits the readiness level of the child.

Numeracy encompasses mastery of the basic symbols and processes of arithmetic, along with the ability to reason with numbers and other mathematical concepts. In recent years, studies have confirmed the importance of basic numeracy for learning success in advanced mathematics achievement (Halberda, Mazzocco, and Feigenson 2008). Unfortunately, more children are coming to school without basic numeracy experiences and skills and, consequently, are struggling to understand the mathematics instruction teachers are expected to deliver.

Number sense is a predictor of success in learning mathematics. For most early childhood educators, this is not news. Montessori, Piaget, Vygotsky, and other pioneers of early childhood learning have emphasized the need to build on basic skills and instruct at each child's level of readiness in order to optimize learning outcomes (Lillard 2005; Pass 2004). Locuniak and Jordan (2008) have shown that kindergarten number sense can predict second-grade math skills. Lembke et al. (2008) have demonstrated standard measures of progress for early numeracy that predict long-term success in math. Clements and Serama (2009) have described the trajectory effect of early learning experiences in math. Griffin (2004), Berch (2005), and other researchers emphasize the importance of developing deep understanding of essential number skills and concepts.

> The basic motor skills in this book are the foundation skills that allow for active lives and help stimulate optimal brain growth and development in the early years.

With this activity book, you can see the sequence of skills that lead to solid numeracy, determine gaps in a child's development of numeracy, and then match activities to his needs and readiness. The sequence of skills in the Numeracy Skills Profile allows you to determine whether the child is at a *Beginning*, *Developing*, or *Proficient* level. Once you establish which skills are already solid (proficient), you will be able to focus on the skills that are developing and ready to be learned. This is sometimes called *tiered* instruction—building upon previously established skills. Instruction at a child's level of readiness is delivered for as long as it takes to develop the understanding that's needed to truly appreciate and enjoy mathematical learning. Using the activities in this section will also ensure that children develop a thorough understanding of the number concepts and applications described in the National Curriculum Standards. Children who deeply understand and enjoy math will have the foundation to continue to expand their knowledge of mathematics. And it is this foundation that enables the child to excel in math throughout school and beyond.

Gross motor skills are another essential aspect of early childhood development. The basic motor skills described in this book are not sufficient to turn children into Olympians or professional athletes; instead, they are the foundation skills that allow for active lives and help stimulate optimal brain growth and development in the early years. The importance of these primary motor skills is well described in the literature (Hannaford 2005; Liddle and Yorke 2003), as is the importance of exercise and cardiovascular fitness (Ratey 2008).

Unfortunately, children's physical activity levels have decreased in recent decades and few children are exercising at the recommended levels (Corbin and Pangrazi 1992; Greene and Adeyanju 1991; Kuntzleman 1993; McGinnis 1987). Richard Louv describes a nation of sedentary children, isolated by technology and video entertainment, who have lost their connection to nature and play (Louv 2005). As a result, a growing number of children are entering school with poor or delayed motor skill development (Liddle and Yorke 2003; Pica 2004). This deficiency may affect movement, attention, listening, visual motor skills, visual perceptual skills, and behavior and social skills (Liddle and Yorke 2003; Hannaford 2005). In addition, more children are being diagnosed with sensory processing disorders, speech development delays, and learning disabilities (Ayres, Robbins, and McAfee 2005; Kranowitz 2005).

Many experienced early childhood educators can remember when building basic motor skills was included in the curriculum. But today, the time devoted to building movement skills has decreased as the emphasis on improving standardized test scores has increased. So the second part of the book focuses on helping you carefully assess whether children have the essential gross motor skills they need, and shows how you can provide instruction and practice until these skills are fully developed.

As in the numeracy skills section, the sequence of skills in the Gross Motor Skills Profile enables you to assess the level of each child—*Beginning*, *Developing*, or *Proficient*—and then focus on the skills that need to be learned. Each skill is accompanied by a variety of activities, arranged from basic to challenging, so that you can provide the most effective learning experiences at the correct instructional level.

While the essential math and movement skills may seem easy enough to teach and learn, it is important to recognize that many schools (a) expect all children to be ready to learn skills at the same level, (b) pace instruction with little opportunity for variance, (c) encourage teachers to move on in the curriculum even when they know several children do not yet understand the material, and (d) do little to encourage careful formative assessment or the use of manipulatives as teaching aids.

Educators who are determined to teach well face the challenge of finding the time to carefully assess the children's readiness, deliver instruction at the appropriate level of readiness, develop meaningful relationships with children, help them understand the value of learning, and build a culture of safety and respect within the classroom.

Both sections of this book begin with three charts: a developmental skills profile, a rubric for determining level of development, and a chart of procedures to use for assessment. Since the skills are organized in a developmental sequence, generally you will build proficiency in skills at the beginning of the list before moving on to more advanced skills. Several activities are included with each skill, enabling you to plan learning so that the child can be successful and you can maximize both learning and joy. The standard for a good instructional match is 95 percent success; use this as a guide to choosing activities that are great matches for the needs of each child.

> Children learn best
> By spending time on-task
> At the appropriate instructional level
> In a safe place
> Doing meaningful work
> With a teacher they love.

When children start working on a skill but are at the early stages of development, you can mark them as *Beginning* (record the date when you began working on this skill). Using the rubric as a guide, you will observe their skills improving to the level indicated as *Developing* (record the date). When they reach *Proficient* status, record the date, celebrate, and move on to the activities that support another skill.

If you are working within the structure of a Responsive Instruction or Response to Intervention initiative, the Numeracy and Gross Motor Skills Profiles serve as diagnostic assessments that allow you to record the skill levels of the children and determine any gaps in their development. You can plan instruction with this baseline data in mind (formative assessment and planning). As children build skills, you will monitor progress and indicate on the skills profile (with a date) when they achieve developing or proficient status (progress monitoring). The developmental skills profiles give you the assessment tools you need to determine skill levels, plan precise instruction based on each child's readiness, and monitor progress toward proficiency for every skill within the sequence.

Please keep in mind that learning these skills is not a race. Children develop at different rates and have different learning experiences at home and school. It is far less important to move quickly through the sequence of skills than it is to fully develop each one, provide joyful early learning experiences, and carefully build a solid foundation based on every skill described in the developmental skills profiles.

This book provides you with a framework for giving each child exactly what she needs in order to develop solid skills and thereby experience joy and success, fall in love with learning, and prepare to be a lifelong learner.

Thank you for being the adult who allows children to learn essential skills at each one's level of readiness.

Thank you for being the adult who helps children build every skill, so there are no weak points in the foundation for learning.

Thank you for nurturing the successful experiences that help children learn to believe in themselves as effective learners for life.

Teach with joy,

Bob Sornson, PhD

President, Early Learning Foundation

# Section 1: Numeracy Skills

# Numeracy Skills Profile

Student: _____   Date of Birth: _____

Teacher: _____   Grade: _____   School: _____

Skill

|  | Beginning | Developing | Proficient |
|---|---|---|---|

- Counts steps aloud with accuracy (to 10).
- Counts objects aloud with accuracy (to 10).
- Models gross motor patterns.
- Models basic fine motor patterns.
- Builds/draws objects that reflect an understanding of relative size.
- Replicates patterns when building or drawing.
- Creates patterns when building or drawing.
- Estimates distance (by taking steps, using blocks, etc.).
- Combines objects (beanbags, marbles, beads, etc.) to make a greater number.
- Counts objects aloud with accuracy (to 100).
- Understands concepts of add on and take away (using manipulatives).
- Recognizes number groups to 10 without counting every object.
- Shows groups of objects to correctly represent numbers to 10.
- Adds on or takes away from a group (to 10).
- Recognizes number groups to 100 without counting every object.
- Shows groups of objects by number (to 100).
- Adds on or takes away from a group (to 100).
- Identifies place values (ones, tens, hundreds, thousands).
- Skip counts with manipulatives to a multiple of 10.
- Solves basic math problems using manipulatives, then transfers the problems to paper.

REPRODUCIBLE

# Numeracy Skills Rubric

| Skill | Beginning | Developing | Proficient |
|---|---|---|---|
| Counts steps aloud with accuracy (to 10). | Counts fewer than 5 steps aloud. | Counts 5–9 steps aloud. | Counts 10 steps aloud. |
| Counts objects aloud with accuracy (to 10). | Counts fewer than 5 objects aloud. | Counts 5–9 objects aloud. | Counts 10 objects aloud. |
| Models gross motor patterns. | Struggles to model gross motor patterns. | Copies 2- to 3-step gross motor patterns most of the time. | Easily copies 3-step gross motor patterns. |
| Models basic fine motor patterns. | Struggles to model 2-step tapping, patting, or clapping patterns. | Copies 2- to 3-step tapping, patting, or clapping patterns most of the time. | Easily copies 4-step tapping, patting, or clapping patterns. |
| Builds/draws objects that reflect an understanding of relative size. | Builds/draws partial objects (might need some guidance and/or modeling) that do not reflect an understanding of relative size. | Builds/draws objects (might need some guidance and/or modeling) that begin to reflect an understanding of relative size. | Builds/draws objects that reflect an understanding of relative size. |
| Replicates patterns when building or drawing. | Beginning to replicate patterns when building or drawing objects (usually needs some guidance and/or modeling). | Replicates 2- to 3-part patterns when building or drawing objects most of the time (might need some guidance and/or modeling). | Replicates 4-part patterns when building or drawing objects most of the time. |
| Creates patterns when building or drawing. | Beginning to create 2-part patterns when building or drawing (might need some guidance and/or modeling). | Creates 3-part patterns when building or drawing (might need some guidance and/or modeling). | Creates 4-part patterns when building or drawing most of the time. |
| Estimates distance (by taking steps, using blocks, etc.). | Estimates distance but needs modeling and guidance. | Estimates distance some of the time. May need guidance and modeling. | Accurately estimates distance consistently without guidance or modeling. |

REPRODUCIBLE

| | | | |
|---|---|---|---|
| Combines objects (beanbags, marbles, beads, etc.) to make a greater number. | Combines objects to make a value of 5 or less. | Combines objects to make a value up to 9. | Combines objects to make a value of 10 or more. |
| Counts objects aloud with accuracy (to 100). | Counts objects with accuracy up to 10, with assistance. | Counts objects with accuracy up to 50. | Counts objects with accuracy to 100. |
| Understands concepts of add on and take away (using manipulatives). | Has difficulty understanding concepts of add on and take away. Requires assistance when working with manipulatives. | Understands add on and take away and can demonstrate greater than or less than, using manipulatives. | Understands add on and take away and can quickly add or take away 1 or 2 from a set of objects with a value up to 10 using manipulatives. |
| Recognizes number groups to 10 without counting every object. | Struggles to quickly recognize number groups to 5. Must count objects to recognize the number value. | Recognizes number groups to 10 with assistance. | Independently and quickly recognizes number groups to 10. |
| Shows groups of objects to correctly represent numbers to 10. | Struggles to quickly and accurately show number groups to 5. Must count objects to demonstrate the number value. | Chooses the correct number of objects to show a number value up to 10 most of the time. | Independently and quickly chooses the correct number of objects to show a number value to 10. |
| Adds on or takes away from a group (to 10). | Has difficulty combining or taking away objects to make a value of 10 or less. Needs to count to recognize the sum or difference. | Can slowly combine objects to make a value of 10 or less and take away using numbers up to 10. Often needs to count objects to check value. | Consistently and quickly combines objects to make any value of 10 or less and takes away using numbers up to 10. |
| Recognizes number groups to 100 without counting every object. | Recognizes number groups with/without counting every object up to 20. May need some guidance or modeling. | Recognizes number groups with/without counting every object up to 100. Sometimes needs guidance. | Consistently and independently recognizes number groups to 100 without counting every object. |

| | | | |
|---|---|---|---|
| Shows groups of objects by number (to 100). | Shows number groups with/without counting every object up to 20. May need some guidance or modeling. | Shows number groups with/without counting every object up to 100. Sometimes needs guidance. | Consistently and independently shows number groups to 100 without counting every object. |
| Adds on or takes away from a group (to 100). | Combines objects to make a value of 10 or less and takes away using numbers up to 10. | Combines objects to make a value of 100 or less and takes away using numbers up to 100, but is still slow, over-relies on counting, and needs support. | Consistently and independently combines objects to make a value of 100 or less and takes away using numbers up to 100. |
| Identifies place values (ones, tens, hundreds, thousands). | Does not yet consistently and correctly identify ones and tens. | Correctly identifies ones, tens, and hundreds. Some inconsistency is noted. | Consistently and correctly identifies ones, tens, hundreds, and thousands. |
| Skip counts with manipulatives to a multiple of 10. | Skip counts by 5 & 10, using manipulatives, to a multiple of 10. May need some guidance. | Skip counts by 2, 3, 4, 5 & 10, using manipulatives, to a multiple of 10. | Consistently skip counts by 2, 3, 4, 5, 6, 7, 8, 9 & 10 with manipulatives. |
| Solves basic math problems using manipulatives, then transfers the problems to paper. | Solves addition and subtraction problems with manipulatives, using numbers to 20 and then solves the same problems on paper. | Solves addition and subtraction problems with manipulatives, using numbers to 100 and then solves the same problems on paper. Shows grouping problems using manipulatives. | Solves addition, subtraction, multiplication, and division problems with manipulatives, using numbers to 100 and then solves the same problems on paper. |

REPRODUCIBLE

# Procedures for Assessment of Numeracy Skills

| Skill | Procedures for Assessment | Standards for Proficiency |
|---|---|---|
| Counts steps aloud with accuracy (to 10). | Have the child count 10 steps without prompts or assistance. | Counts 10 steps aloud. |
| Counts objects aloud with accuracy (to 10). | Have the child count 10 objects (coins, beads, chips, rocks, etc.) without prompts or assistance. | Counts 10 objects aloud. |
| Models gross motor patterns. | After watching you model a 3-step pattern (e.g., *step forward/raise both hands/step left*), the child copies your steps in the correct order. | Easily copies 3-step gross motor patterns. |
| Models basic fine motor patterns. | After watching you model a 4-step pattern (e.g., *tap right hand twice on table/clap both hands together twice/tap left hand twice on the table/clap both hands together twice*), the child copies your steps in the correct order. | Easily copies 4-step tapping, patting, or clapping patterns. |
| Builds/draws objects that reflect an understanding of relative size. | Have the child draw a picture of a house and the yard around the house. Analyze the drawing for relative size (for example, is the door proportionate to the windows, is the tree proportionate to the size of the house, etc.?). The picture should reflect general rather than exact proportions. | Builds/draws objects that reflect an understanding of relative size. |
| Replicates patterns when building or drawing. | Have the child continue an established visual pattern, using colors or shapes (for example, 1 red circle, 2 blue circles, 1 green circle, 3 black circles; *or* rectangle, circle, square, triangle). | Replicates 4-part patterns when building or drawing objects most of the time. |
| Creates patterns when building or drawing. | Have the child build a pattern using colored pattern blocks and then explain it to you so you can continue the pattern. The pattern should have at least 4 elements. | Creates 4-part patterns when building or drawing most of the time. |

REPRODUCIBLE

| | | |
|---|---|---|
| Estimates distance (by taking steps, using blocks, etc.). | Have the child estimate how many steps it will take to get from where she is presently standing to a destination that is within 5–15 steps (for example, "How many steps will it take you to get to the door?"). | Accurately estimates distance consistently without guidance or modeling. |
| Combines objects (beanbags, marbles, beads, etc.) to make a greater number. | Ask the child to take ___ red beads and ___ blue beads and then describe the total number of beads. Allow recounting if needed. | Combines objects to make a value of 10 or more. |
| Counts objects aloud with accuracy to 100. | Using a counting frame or abacus, have the child count various sets of beads, using numbers up to 100. Assess based on accuracy, not speed. | Counts objects with accuracy to 100. |
| Understands concepts of add on and take away using manipulatives. | Using a counting frame or abacus, have the child identify a number group made up of beads (1–10) and then quickly recognize the result of adding on or taking away 1, 2, or 3. | Understands add on and take away and can quickly add or take away 1 or 2 from a set of objects with a value up to 10 using manipulatives. |
| Recognizes number groups to 10 without counting every object. | Using a counting frame or abacus, have the child quickly identify (within 3 seconds and without having to count beads individually) any number between 1 and 10. | Independently and quickly recognizes number groups to 10. |
| Shows groups of objects to correctly represent numbers to 10. | Using a counting frame or abacus, have the child quickly (within 3 seconds and without having to count beads individually) show the correct number of beads representing numerals between 1 and 10. | Independently and quickly chooses the correct number of objects to show a number value to 10. |
| Adds on or takes away from a group (to 10). | Using a counting frame or abacus, have the child quickly (within 3 seconds) show a number of beads, then quickly add on or take away a value from this number. | Consistently and quickly combines objects to make any value of 10 or less and takes away using numbers up to 10. |
| Recognizes number groups to 100 without counting every object. | Using a counting frame or abacus, have the child recognize numbers displayed, using numbers from 1 to 100. Child should be able to recognize even larger numbers within 10 seconds. | Consistently and independently recognizes number groups to 100 without counting every object. |

REPRODUCIBLE

| | | |
|---|---|---|
| Shows groups of objects by number (to 100). | Using a counting frame or abacus, have the child display any number from 1 to 100. Child should be able to display even larger numbers within 10 seconds. | Consistently and independently shows number groups to 100 without counting every object. |
| Adds on or takes away from a group (to 100). | Using a counting frame or abacus, have the child display any number from 1 to 100, then add on or take away any number less than 100. | Consistently and independently combines objects to make a value of 100 or less and takes away using numbers up to 100. |
| Identifies place values (ones, tens, hundreds, thousands). | Using a number displayed on paper, have the child identify the ones, tens, hundreds, and thousands places. Have the child identify the place and number value in each column. | Consistently and correctly identifies ones, tens, hundreds, and thousands. |
| Skip counts with manipulatives to a multiple of 10. | Using a counting frame or abacus, have the child count by ___, up to a multiple of 10, and show that value on the abacus while counting (for example, when saying 3, there should be 3 beads shown; when saying 6, there should be 6 beads shown). | Consistently skip counts by 2, 3, 4, 5, 6, 7, 8, 9 & 10 with manipulatives. |
| Solves basic math problems using manipulatives, then transfers the problems to paper. | Have the child solve basic math problems (addition to 100, subtraction within 100, multiplication and division using numbers not exceeding 100) on the abacus, and then show the same problems and solution on paper. | Solves addition, subtraction, multiplication, and division problems using numbers to 100 with manipulatives, and then solves the same problems on paper. |

# Activities for Building NUMERACY SKILLS

Research of the past decade or so indicates more clearly than ever that educators of young children need to encourage numeracy in ways other than the memorization of facts and formulas. For children to be successful in their mathematical lives, they need to have many opportunities to search for sense and meaning, explore patterns and relationships, and understand the order and the predictability of numbers and number groups. A deeper numerical understanding not only affects a child's success in mathematics but also has a positive impact on other areas of the curriculum. Encouraging numeracy development through play, independent exploration, and experimentation will benefit children in their early and essential numeracy skills development and, at the same time, lessen their anxiety and negative attitudes toward mathematics as school demands become more complex.

**Skill:** Counts steps aloud with accuracy (to 10).

The understanding of basic number values must be grounded in the experience of feeling, seeing, saying, and hearing the sequence of numbers. Counting while moving the body develops a deep kinesthetic understanding of what it feels like to move 3 steps compared to 10 steps. This is an essential component of number sense.

# Guided Tour

BEGINNING

INDIVIDUAL OR SMALL GROUP

Have the child choose a destination within a designated space that he'd like to walk to that's no more than 10 steps away. Walk to that point together, counting steps in unison as you go. When you've reached the destination, you (or another child, if working with a small group) can choose the next destination and repeat the process. As the child becomes more skilled, have him travel from place to place on his own, counting steps aloud as he goes.

# Down the Garden Path

BEGINNING

INDIVIDUAL

Draw one to five dots on five plastic stepping spots and place them on the floor in a path in numerical order. Each spot represents the value of the numeral written on it. Hold the hand of the child you are working with, and ask him to walk next to you and count out loud from 1 to 5 as he goes from spot to spot. Increase the number of stepping spots to 10 once the child experiences success with the smaller numbers.

Number Facts & Jumping Jacks

# Follow My Lead

INDIVIDUAL

BEGINNING

Take a certain number of steps and then ask the child to take the same number of steps. For example, if you take three steps, she should follow your lead and take three steps. Count your steps to yourself but have the child count hers aloud. Start out with a small number, such as three or four, and increase the number as she becomes more successful.

# Step-Scotch

INDIVIDUAL

BEGINNING

Create a traditional hopscotch pattern, with or without the numbers, using tape or chalk. Give the child a beanbag and ask her to throw it onto one of the sections. Have her step on each section, counting her steps out loud as she retrieves the beanbag after each throw.

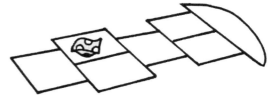

# Throw and Go

BEGINNING/DEVELOPING

SMALL GROUP (in the classroom)
OR WHOLE GROUP (in a gymnasium or outside)

Bring the children to an open space, give each one a beanbag (or koosh ball), and ask them to throw theirs underhand, away from their bodies. Then have them count the number of steps they must take to retrieve their beanbags. Let the children do this simultaneously as you move around to check on their progress. Repeat the activity, encouraging them to throw farther the next time to increase the number of steps (and counting) it will take to retrieve their beanbags.

# By the Numbers

**INDIVIDUAL**

BEGINNING/DEVELOPING

Write numbers from 1 to 10 on index cards, one number per card. Place the cards in an opaque bag and ask the child to draw one. Tell him to read the number on the card and take that number of steps before returning to you and drawing another card. You can vary this activity by asking the child to show the number with hops, skips, claps, or knee slaps.

# In Step

**INDIVIDUAL, SMALL GROUP, OR WHOLE GROUP**

DEVELOPING

Pick out some places you can walk to in your classroom. Then ask the children to help you count the number of steps it takes for *you* to get from the door to the desk, for example. After the number has been determined, ask a few children to see how many steps it takes them to follow the same path (from the door to the desk). Then move on to another spot (from the desk to the window perhaps), with the children counting your steps and then theirs.

# From Place to Place

**INDIVIDUAL**

DEVELOPING

Set up a combination of different markers (coffee cans filled with sand, plastic safety cones, carpet squares, etc.) around your work space, placing them a few feet apart from each other. Ask the child to travel from one marker to another, counting his steps aloud as he travels and announcing how many steps it took him to get to a marker. Listen to his counting to see if it's accurate, and if it isn't, make note of where he went out of order. As he becomes successful, move the markers farther apart until it takes the child about 10 steps to get from one to another.

# Number Ladders

INDIVIDUAL OR
SMALL GROUP

Use masking tape to make one or more ladders, each with 10 "rungs," on the floor of your work space. Ask the children to start at one end of a ladder and "climb" it, counting steps out loud as they go. For a greater challenge, have them to do it in reverse, counting backward to 1.

DEVELOPING

# Every Which Way

SMALL GROUP OR
WHOLE GROUP

Have the children take different kinds of steps (giant, baby, on tiptoe, on heels, backward, sideways, etc.) as they move toward destinations or markers around your work area. Tell them to count each step they take out loud.

DEVELOPING/PROFICIENT

# Skill: Counts objects aloud with accuracy (to 10).

The ability to count with accuracy is critical. It is a life skill everyone needs in order to be effective not only in schoolwork but also in life—dealing with money, buying groceries, following recipes, setting up appointments, and so on. Start developing this skill using the numbers 1 to 10 to build an understanding of basic number patterns and number values.

## One to Ten

BEGINNING

**INDIVIDUAL**

Place 10 small plastic cups numbered from 1 to 10 in front of the child and give him a pile of beads or buttons. Tell him to place the same number of beads or buttons in each cup as the number written on the cup. Check each cup with the child by dumping out the contents and counting the items aloud together.

## Roll and Count

BEGINNING

**INDIVIDUAL, SMALL GROUP, OR**
**WHOLE GROUP (in pairs)**

Give each child a die and 10 counting chips. Tell her to roll the die and determine the number she's rolled. Then have her count out that number of chips. Verify her accuracy. Next, you take a turn. Roll the die, count out that number of chips, and let *her* make sure *you* are right. Continue alternating turns. If children are playing in pairs, one partner rolls and counts out chips, and the other checks the first child's accuracy. Then they switch roles.

# Ten Apples

INDIVIDUAL

DEVELOPING

Give the child a copy of the book *Ten Apples Up On Top* and 10 or more red counting chips. Have her go to a page of her choice, count the apples on top of an animal's head, and count out the same number of red chips. Repeat the process with other pages in the book.

# I Spy

INDIVIDUAL

DEVELOPING

Provide the child with an *I Spy* book or any other book that has a number of different objects on each page. Turn to one of the pages, choose an object, and ask the child to tell you how many there are, counting aloud as he goes. Repeat with other objects on the page or at another place in the book.

# A Graph About You

INDIVIDUAL, SMALL GROUP, OR WHOLE GROUP

DEVELOPING

Give each child a crayon or marker, a blank 12 x 12 grid on a piece of paper, and a small mirror (optional). With your help if necessary, have each child create a personal graph that shows how many eyes, fingers, elbows, toes, ears, and feet she has. She is responsible for counting her toes, for example, and then counting out the corresponding number of boxes, which she will then color on the graph (in this case 10).

# Pile It On

**DEVELOPING**

INDIVIDUAL OR SMALL GROUP

Collect a number of items from around the classroom (erasers, crayons, blocks, puzzle pieces, etc.), making sure there are multiples but no more than 10 of every item. Give each child several of each item. Tell the child to first sort the items into piles with the same items and then count how many are in each pile. Children in a small group can exchange materials and repeat the process.

# Show Me the Money

**DEVELOPING/PROFICIENT**

INDIVIDUAL OR SMALL GROUP

Give the child a pile of pennies and a game spinner that has five sections on it, each section containing a different number between one and five. Have the child spin the spinner and count out the number of pennies that corresponds to the number the spinner landed on. Ask her to spin it again, count out that number of pennies, and then determine how many pennies she has counted out all together. Keep playing until she reaches the target number (any number up to and including 10 that you determine). Children playing in pairs or small groups can take turns spinning the spinner and counting out pennies, trying to reach or exceed the target number before their opponent.

# Counting in Your Mind

**DEVELOPING/PROFICIENT**

INDIVIDUAL OR SMALL GROUP

Show the child a tray on which you have placed several objects, for example, red blocks, blue marbles, green bows, etc. Tell the child to study the objects on the tray for 10 seconds, and then cover it with a towel. Have the child tell you how many red blocks were on the tray, remove the towel, and have her count to see if she was correct. Repeat the procedure and ask her to tell you the number of blue marbles, for example. Keep it fun and successful. In a small group, ask different children, "How many were there?" each time.

# Skill: Models gross motor patterns.

Modeling gross motor patterns involves the whole body, which is great for your tactile/kinesthetic learners. Developing this skill deepens a child's understanding of patterns by bringing the concept into a three-dimensional realm. It is important for children to realize that while patterns frequently occur on pieces of paper in school, they also extend well beyond the classroom and into music, play, dancing, exercise, and daily locomotion.

## One Foot in Front of the Other

BEGINNING

INDIVIDUAL

Bring the child to an open space where you and she can walk several steps in any direction without running into anything. Have her stand next to you. Take one step forward and tell her to copy you. Take one step to the side and, again, have her copy the movement. Continue taking single steps in a variety of directions and asking her to copy them. Once she becomes successful doing one-step tasks, increase to two steps. At first, do the same step twice and then introduce a sequence of two different steps (forward, backward; to the side, on toes; on heels, toes pointing in; etc.). Don't make it too challenging, as you want to establish a high success rate and keep it within the child's reach.

## One at a Time

BEGINNING

INDIVIDUAL OR SMALL GROUP

Face the children and do one simple gross motor task, like tapping your head or clapping your hands. Once they've watched you, ask the children to copy what you just did. After several successful rounds, move onto slightly more complicated one-part tasks, such as making forward arm circles or lifting one leg briefly. Finally, do more challenging tasks such as stepping backwards or touching one elbow to the opposite knee. Each time you ask the children to do something new, be sure to model that movement for them.

# One Side Then Two

INDIVIDUAL OR
SMALL GROUP

BEGINNING

Begin with simple gross motor patterns that require the children to use only one side of their body. Examples include raising one hand up in the air, touching the right hand to the right cheek, sticking the elbow out to the side, and lifting one foot onto its heel. As children become proficient at copying your one-sided, one-part movements, try others that will require them to cross the midline of their body, such as moving the right hand to the left knee, the left hand to the right elbow, the right hand to the left shoulder, and crossing the left foot over the right foot.

# Going Through Hoops

INDIVIDUAL

BEGINNING/DEVELOPING

Place a hula hoop on the floor and ask the child to watch what you do. Walk around the hoop once and then step inside it. Have him copy you. For the next sequence, you might start inside the hoop, take one step forward, and then hop over the rim of the hoop. Continue with simple one- and two-part sequences. As his skill improves, ask the child to copy more complicated gross motor sequences.

# Patty-Cake in Parts

INDIVIDUAL

DEVELOPING

Stand facing the child and begin doing the motions for and saying the words to the patty-cake rhyme very slowly, one or two movements at a time. Tell the child to copy you after each set of movements you show him. When you get to the "roll it, knead it, mark it with a B" part, get creative with the motions and make each one of those a separate movement that the child will copy.

# Animals in Action

INDIVIDUAL, SMALL GROUP,
OR WHOLE GROUP

DEVELOPING

Have the children help you create actions that represent different animals. For example, you might flap your arms like a bird, waddle like a penguin, or gallop like a horse. Once a repertoire of actions has been established, do two or three in a sequence and have the children copy you. Other animal actions might include a chicken pecking, a cat clawing, a fish swimming, a dog digging, a snake slithering, a rabbit hopping, and an elephant lumbering.

# Two Back at You

INDIVIDUAL

DEVELOPING

Face the child and show her a sequence of two simple gross motor tasks, such as stepping forward and then clapping your hands. Tell her to copy you. Next, have her copy a different sequence, like tapping your knees and then raising both hands. Repeat until the child is successful in copying a number of two-part sequences that vary in difficulty. If desired, allow her to make up some of the sequences herself.

# Opposites

INDIVIDUAL, SMALL GROUP, OR
WHOLE GROUP

DEVELOPING

Ask the children to face you and copy the opposing motions you show them. Use verbal cues to reinforce the math vocabulary as you demonstrate. For example, make movements with your arms or body that represent big and small. At the same time, say the words "big" and "small." Then have the children copy you. Next, demonstrate tall and short, and have the children copy you again. Other opposite pairs might be wide and narrow, high and low, over and under, even and odd (using finger patterns), behind and in front of, and more and less.

# Follow the Leader

**INDIVIDUAL, SMALL GROUP, OR WHOLE GROUP**

DEVELOPING

Play a semitraditional game of Follow the Leader with the children. At first, just do one action, such as patting the top of your head, and have the children copy you. Continue with other one-part tasks, making them more challenging as you go. Once children are successful with one, try two-part gross motor patterns, such as stepping forward and then tapping your knees with your hands. Again ask the children to copy you. As they become skilled at copying difficult two-part patterns, challenge them by adding a third task.

# Triple Play

**INDIVIDUAL**

DEVELOPING/PROFICIENT

In your work space, set up a path with three objects in close proximity to each other. You might use a hula hoop, a carpet square, and a plastic stepping spot, for example. Have the child watch you make your way along the path. At first, you might do the same thing with each object, like walking around or hopping on each one. Whatever you choose, have the child copy you exactly. Once he is successful copying one motion, try doing two different things as you move along the path, such as walking *around* the hoop, stepping *on* the square, and walking *around* the stepping spot. As his skill in copying you increases, do three different things: walk *around* the hoop, step *on* the carpet square, and hop two-legged *onto* the stepping spot.

# Gross Motor Pattern Play

**INDIVIDUAL OR SMALL GROUP**

DEVELOPING/PROFICIENT

In this activity, the children copy gross motor patterns that require moving their entire bodies. You might start out with a two-part sequence of hopping on one foot and then doing one jumping jack. As the children become more skilled, increase the difficulty and number of actions in the sequence you want them to copy. Other actions include skipping, galloping, marching, walking backward, jumping, hopping on two legs, and jumping from one foot to the other.

## Skill: Models basic fine motor patterns.

Traditionally, we think of fine motor skills in relation to writing, cutting, drawing, tying, etc. Bringing these little muscles into the world of mathematics will be a new idea for some educators. Just like some of the other skills in this section, developing this one will add another level of complexity to a child's understanding of patterns.

## Trumpet Playing

BEGINNING

INDIVIDUAL

Model how to touch your pointer finger to your thumb. Then show how to touch your thumb to each of your fingers. Allow the child to practice moving his fingers in that fashion on his own for a minute or so. Then ask the child to watch what you do and copy you. Touch any one fingertip to the tip of your thumb and quickly release. Ask the child to do the same. Try another finger/thumb combination, asking the child to copy you each time. Eventually, do a two-part sequence and have the child copy you.

## Raggedy Wrists

BEGINNING

INDIVIDUAL OR
SMALL GROUP

Sit at a table of the appropriate height facing the children. Place your elbows on the table and keep your hands erect. Ask the children to do the same. Let one of your wrists flop forward and then bring it back to its original position. Have each child copy you. Repeat with the other wrist. Next, let one wrist flop backward and have the children copy you. Repeat with the other wrist. Demonstrate a wrist twist and then bring it back to its original position. Once children are able to do those movements with ease, model combinations of the movements with one or both hands for them to copy.

# Follow My Fingers

**INDIVIDUAL, SMALL GROUP, OR WHOLE GROUP**

BEGINNING

Face the children and ask them to copy whatever you do with your fingers. Hold up any one (appropriate) finger and have them copy you. Repeat with other individual fingers. Then hold up multiple fingers, like the pointer and the middle finger or the thumb and the pointer, and have the children copy you. Continue with one-part and then two-part sequences, asking the children to copy you after each sequence.

# Twofer

**INDIVIDUAL OR SMALL GROUP**

BEGINNING/DEVELOPING

Sit on the floor facing the child. Show him a two-part fine motor sequence such as tapping your right hand once on the floor, then bringing both hands together in front of you. Have the child copy your movements. Do another two-part sequence: tapping your right hand on the floor and then your left hand on the floor. Again, tell him to copy you. Continue with other two-part sequences, increasing the complexity and using both hands as the child becomes more skilled.

# Tappers

**INDIVIDUAL**

DEVELOPING

Sit at a table of the appropriate height facing the child. Place both hands flat on the table in front of you, fingers spread out, and ask him to do the same. Show him how to lift one finger at a time off the table without raising the rest of the hand. Tell him to copy you, using his dominant hand, and let him practice for a while. Once he's comfortable, model two- and three-part sequences you want him to copy, such as lifting and tapping your pointer finger twice, your pinky finger once, and your thumb twice. Add the fingers on the other hand when he's ready for something more challenging.

# Fine Motor Charades

**INDIVIDUAL**

DEVELOPING

Create a list of fine motor actions that the child is familiar with, such as writing, waving, eating, turning a doorknob, and cutting. Choose one to start with and act it out with a very brief, deliberate movement. After you've shown the child, ask her to guess what you were acting out and to copy what you just did. Repeat with other one-handed fine motor tasks. As she becomes better able to copy you, expand to two-handed fine motor tasks, like buttoning, tying, playing piano, or putting on gloves.

# Rock, Paper, Scissors

**INDIVIDUAL**

DEVELOPING/PROFICIENT

This is a twist on the traditional game of Rock, Paper, Scissors. Model for the child each of the three hand symbols (a fist for "rock," a flat hand for "paper," and two fingers out straight for "scissors") and ask her to demonstrate each one. Then begin showing her random three-part combinations of the symbols, such as *rock, rock, paper* or *paper, scissors, rock*. After each sequence, have the child copy you. Use verbal cues along with the hand signals at first, then eliminate the verbal cues as the child becomes more skilled.

# Nap, Tap, Lap, and Clap

**INDIVIDUAL, SMALL GROUP, OR WHOLE GROUP**

DEVELOPING/PROFICIENT

Model what each movement looks like: nap – hands together with your head resting on them; tap – openhanded tapping with flat hands; lap – touching your lap with your hands; and clap – clapping hands in the traditional manner. Now have the children copy you after you do each one. Do the actions again but in random, three-part combinations like *nap, lap, clap,* and have them copy you again. As they are successful with three parts, try some similar four-part patterns.

NUMERACY SKILLS

# Skill: Builds/draws objects that reflect an understanding of relative size.

It is vital for children to understand that math runs rampant (in a good way!) throughout our world, not just in our classrooms. The relationships we perceive between objects in our environment inform us about weight, height, length, value, and how we interact with them. Conversations with children, early and often, are crucial here. Encourage parents to talk to their child about the sizes of things during everyday tasks and routines—the opportunities are endless. This concept helps build the foundation for understanding ratios, proportion, slope, angle, geometry, probability, and statistics.

## A House Is a House

BEGINNING

INDIVIDUAL, SMALL GROUP,
OR WHOLE GROUP

Find a picture of a house with a yard and show it to the children. Discuss what they see around the house. Then ask them to point out some things that are bigger than the house itself (trees, another house or building, etc.). Next, ask the children to identify things that are smaller than the house (shrubs, cars, people). Finally, have them look at the house itself and direct their attention to the fact that the windows and doors are smaller than the house and closer in size to each other. Any other observations they relay about relative size are valuable, so encourage children to express their ideas.

## Big, Bigger, Biggest

BEGINNING

INDIVIDUAL

Give the child three items that vary noticeably in size, such as three blocks, three stuffed animals, or three books. Tell him to arrange them in order from small to large or from large to small. Once he's skilled at doing this, choose items that are closer in size to make it more challenging—like his classmates.

# Me in the Middle

INDIVIDUAL, SMALL GROUP,
OR WHOLE GROUP

BEGINNING

Give each child a piece of paper and some drawing materials. Ask them to draw a ground line (a horizontal line that represents the ground or floor) and then themselves, standing at the center of that line. Next have them draw something bigger than they are to one side of their body. After that, ask them to draw something that is smaller than they are on the other side of their body. When the drawings are complete, talk with them about how much bigger or how much smaller the objects they drew are. For example, a house would be a lot bigger than the child but an adult might be just a little bigger. You might choose to model this procedure for the children before asking them to do it on their own.

# Under Construction I

INDIVIDUAL OR
SMALL GROUP

BEGINNING

Give each child a supply of blocks, a stuffed animal, and some room to work. Ask the children to place their stuffed animals on the floor and to build a block structure next to them that is taller than their stuffed animals. Once that has been done with accuracy, ask the children to build either a new structure or take away some of the blocks to make it much shorter than their stuffed animals. Finally, have them add some blocks so that their structures are about the same size as their stuffed animals.

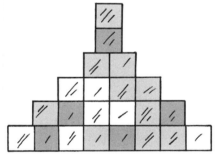

# Under Construction II

BEGINNING/DEVELOPING

INDIVIDUAL OR
SMALL GROUP

Provide each child with several blocks that represent a wide range of sizes. You can include everything from large cardboard "bricks" to tiny cubes. Ask him to build a tower with the blocks, starting with the largest one on the bottom and ending with the smallest on top. At first, you may want to start with just a few blocks, adding more as the child's size discrimination improves.

# Same Size Scavenger Hunt

BEGINNING/DEVELOPING

INDIVIDUAL, SMALL GROUP,
OR WHOLE GROUP

Supply each of the children with a clipboard, paper, and a pencil. Tell them they are going on a scavenger hunt to find things in the room that are about the same size as they are. Once they've found something, they draw it (or write it) on their paper, and then continue to move around the space looking for other things that fit the criteria. Possible answers might be a classmate, bookshelves, an adult's chair, or a filing cabinet. You can vary this activity by having them hunt for things that are about the same size as a computer, a child's shoe, a backpack, and so forth.

# Do You See What I See?

DEVELOPING/PROFICIENT

INDIVIDUAL OR
SMALL GROUP

Sit next to the child so that you both are looking at the same things, or gather a variety of objects in front of you on a tabletop. Play a game of I Spy with the objects in view, and say something like, "I spy with my little eye something that is bigger than my head." Keep in mind that she doesn't need to guess the exact thing you're "spying," just something in view that is bigger than your head. Continue with other objects, being sure to include the terms *smaller than* and *about the same size as*.

# In Real Life

DEVELOPING/PROFICIENT

INDIVIDUAL, SMALL GROUP,
OR WHOLE GROUP

Create a work sheet that has a simple outline of a car at the top. Divide the paper into two columns, one labeled "smaller than" and the other "bigger than." Give each child a copy of the work sheet, scissors, glue, and old magazines or catalogs. Ask them to cut out pictures of things that would be either bigger or smaller than a real-life car and to glue them in the appropriate column on the paper.

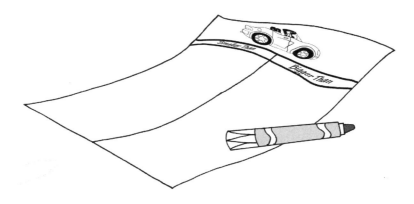

# Skill: Replicates patterns when building or drawing.

Patterns are the foundation of almost every mathematical concept. A child's ability to reproduce patterns is the first of many important patterning skills that will lead not only to spontaneous recognition of more traditional shape and color patterns but also (and even more important) to the eventual recognition of the number and measurement patterns they will use for the rest of their lives.

## Sticky Patterns

BEGINNING

INDIVIDUAL, SMALL GROUP,
OR WHOLE GROUP

Create simple two-part patterns with stickers on sentence strips. Give a strip to each child along with extra stickers. Have the children use their stickers to continue the same pattern on their strips. When they are ready, follow the same procedure with three-part patterns.

## Patterns All Around

BEGINNING

INDIVIDUAL, SMALL GROUP,
OR WHOLE GROUP

Help the children notice how abundant patterns are in our environment. Ask them to take some time to look for patterns around them, such as stripes on a classmate's shirt, colors on playground equipment, patterns in floor tiles, on flowers or leaves, game boards, carpets, windows, and so on. Each time a pattern is found, discuss what characteristics make up the pattern and ask the children to describe it to you.

# Just Hangin' Around

INDIVIDUAL            BEGINNING

Tie a length of clothesline between two objects in your work space and clip some laminated construction-paper shapes to the line to create a two-part pattern. Give the child additional paper shapes and clothespins and have her continue the pattern that you started. Once she's completed it correctly, tell her to remove all of the shapes from the line and then watch as you hang up a new pattern. Have her continue the new pattern. Change patterns as she demonstrates understanding and challenge her by adding a third part when she's ready.

# Hide-and-Seek

INDIVIDUAL            BEGINNING

Gather a supply of pattern blocks. Bring the child to a table or empty floor space and tell him to "hide" his eyes while you make a pattern with some of the blocks. Arrange a two-part pattern with at least four of the blocks. Tell him to open his eyes, "seek" out the pattern, and repeat it using more of the blocks. Once he can do this correctly, ask him to hide his eyes again while you make another pattern, and then repeat the process until success is consistent. Next, create three-part patterns for him to seek.

# Pattern Block Parade

INDIVIDUAL, SMALL GROUP, OR WHOLE GROUP            BEGINNING/DEVELOPING

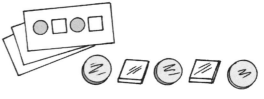

Create two-part patterns by tracing pattern blocks onto sentence strips. Give a strip and a handful of pattern blocks to each child. Have the children use the blocks to replicate the patterns you traced on the strips. As their skills increase, give children three-part pattern strips and repeat the process. Children can trade strips with each other or get other strips from you with different patterns.

# Stamping Sequences

INDIVIDUAL                                                         DEVELOPING

Gather a collection of rubber stamps, an ink pad, and some strips of paper. On each strip, begin a three- or four-part pattern using the stamps. Give a strip to the child and ask her to continue the pattern you started.

# Towers of Patterns

INDIVIDUAL                                                         DEVELOPING

Put out a collection of colored blocks. Have the child watch as you begin to build a tower of stacked blocks in a particular three- or four-part color pattern. After you've built it so the pattern begins to repeat, have the child take over and continue the pattern you have established.

# Pattern Pathways

INDIVIDUAL                                                         DEVELOPING

Bring the child to an open space that has enough room for you to create a path out of plastic stepping spots or carpet squares. Place a stuffed animal where you want the path to end. Create a pathway to the animal by placing the stepping spots in a three-part color pattern. Give the child the rest of the stepping spots and ask her to continue the pathway, using the same color pattern. When she runs out of spots, have her verbalize each color as she takes a step toward the animal at the end of the path. As a variation on this activity, tape or draw shapes on the spots and create shape patterns for the child to use.

# Stackables

INDIVIDUAL OR
SMALL GROUP

DEVELOPING/PROFICIENT

Arrange several stacks of colored plastic cups in different four-part patterns. Give each child a supply of additional cups and have him choose one of the patterned stacks. Tell him to use his cups to continue the pattern that you started stacking. Once he's replicated your pattern one or two times, ask him to set that stack aside, choose a new patterned stack of cups, and repeat the procedure.

# Clippers

INDIVIDUAL OR
SMALL GROUP

DEVELOPING/PROFICIENT

Gather some shoe boxes and a number of different colored plastic clothespins (or use permanent markers to color the ends of wooden clothespins). Make sure to have an assortment of at least four colors. With the clothespins, start a four-part pattern on the edge of a shoe box, creating a different pattern for each box. Have each child sit at a table or on the floor and give her some clothespins and one of the shoe boxes. Tell her to continue the same pattern twice. Once she is successful, have her select another box and do the same with a different pattern.

## Skill: Creates patterns when building or drawing.

After replicating patterns, creating them is the next level of patterning skills. This requires a child to apply the concept, not just recognize it, and that's higher-level thinking. To ensure success, start out with two-part patterns and increase the number of parts as the child becomes more skilled. When developing this skill, don't forget the importance of conversation during your everyday routines. Patterns are everywhere in the environment, but children may not notice them unless they are pointed out to them. Encourage children and their parents to spend time at home creating and discovering patterns in art and play.

## Pattern Chains                                                BEGINNING

INDIVIDUAL, SMALL GROUP,
OR WHOLE GROUP

Model how to link strips of paper to create a chain. Provide each child with tape or glue and a dozen strips of paper, each about one-inch wide and in two different colors. Ask each child to create a two- or three-part pattern by linking her strips together.

## Patterned Parking                                             BEGINNING

INDIVIDUAL

Draw a single row of 12 "parking spaces" on a piece of white construction paper and provide some toy cars in two or three different colors (or draw, color, and cut out car shapes). Ask the child to "park" the cars in a two- or three-part pattern until all of the spaces are full. You can also draw shapes on the cars and have the child create a pattern based on shapes instead of colors.

# Egg-cellent Patterns

**INDIVIDUAL**  BEGINNING

Supply the child with 12 plastic eggs of different colors and an empty, clean egg carton. Ask him to use the eggs to create a two-part pattern in one row of the egg carton. Then have him tell you about the attributes he used to create it (color, orientation, etc.). Then ask him to create another two-part pattern in the other row of the egg carton using different attributes. As a variation, supply the child with a work sheet of egg outlines and ask him to transfer his pattern to the paper by coloring the eggs.

# Socks in a Row

**INDIVIDUAL OR SMALL GROUP**  DEVELOPING

Gather a collection of old but clean socks, making sure that they vary in size, texture, color, and pattern. Talk about the characteristics or attributes of the socks with the children: some have stripes at the top, some are a solid color, some are large, and some are small, etc. Then ask each child to use some of the socks to create a two- or three-part pattern. Ask them to explain their patterns. Once you've checked for understanding, have them create another pattern using other attributes. You can vary this activity by using buttons, for example, and discussing the number of holes, the shape, the size, the color, etc.

# Crazy Caterpillars

**INDIVIDUAL, SMALL GROUP, OR WHOLE GROUP**  DEVELOPING

Give each child a piece of paper, a shapes stencil, and something to trace with. Ask them to make crazy caterpillars by tracing shapes from the stencil in a two- or three-part pattern—for example, square/circle, square/circle or triangle/square/circle, triangle/square/circle. Challenge the children to make more than one crazy caterpillar and to color the caterpillars in a pattern that is different from the one dictated by the shapes.

# I've Been Working on the Railroad

DEVELOPING

INDIVIDUAL, SMALL GROUP, OR WHOLE GROUP

Provide each child with a black-line copy of a train's engine and a number of pattern blocks to serve as the train's cars. Ask them to create a train that is 12 cars long and shows a pattern. Encourage the children to design three-part patterns. Once their patterns are complete and correct, give them each a work sheet with a train's engine on it and ask them to draw the pattern they made with the pattern blocks.

# Snazzy Snakes

DEVELOPING

INDIVIDUAL, SMALL GROUP, OR WHOLE GROUP

Provide each child with crayons, markers, or stickers and an outline of a snake drawn on construction paper. On the snake's back, have each child create a three-part pattern, which can consist of different colors or different shapes, lines, dots, or anything else the children can think of. Ask each child to explain her pattern to make sure she is on the right track before she completes the entire snake.

# Edible Patterns

DEVELOPING

INDIVIDUAL OR SMALL GROUP

Before doing this activity, consult the school nurse (or parents) about any food allergies the children might have. Place several bowls of food items (pretzel sticks, mini-marshmallows, popcorn, raisins, cereal, etc.) on a table in your work space. Give each child a napkin and ask him to open it up and lay it flat on the table in front of him. Then have the children use at least three of the food items to create three- or four-part patterns on their napkins. After they have created their patterns and repeated them, check their accuracy and then let them eat their patterns.

# High-Tech Patterns

INDIVIDUAL

DEVELOPING

Ask the child to create patterns on the computer using the keyboard. She can use numbers, letters, and symbols to create three- and four-part patterns. Encourage her to be creative and to vary the complexity, such as mixing letters and numbers. If you have a clip art program on your computer, she can also use that to create patterns. You may also want to print out children's patterns so they can share and discuss each one.

# Pocket Patterns

INDIVIDUAL

DEVELOPING/PROFICIENT

Secure a pocket chart to a vertical space in your classroom or lay it on the floor. Give the child a collection of paper shapes, both geometric and familiar (dogs, cats, fish, T-shirts, etc.). Have the child place a different shape in each of the chart's pockets to create a pattern and then explain his pattern. Encourage him to go beyond the basics of color and shape and use less traditional attributes such as something that swims, something that flies, something with paws, and so forth.

# Main Street

INDIVIDUAL OR SMALL GROUP

DEVELOPING/PROFICIENT

Create a work sheet that has 10 simple house outlines in a row. Discuss with the child the attributes of houses, for example, what they are made of, the number and shapes of windows, the color of the front door, etc. Then ask the child to design the front of each house on the work sheet to represent a three- or four-part pattern but not necessarily one that is based on color. When she has completed the work sheet, ask her to explain to you what attributes make up the pattern she created.

> **Skill:** Estimates distance (by taking steps, using blocks, etc.).
> We estimate distances and other measurements every day, and we base these estimates on our prior experiential knowledge of distance, weight, length, and so forth. We also use estimates in our conversations with and descriptions to others. Children are accustomed to estimating in the classroom, such as how many pieces of macaroni are in a jar, and by developing this skill, they will deepen their level of understanding of many math concepts. Look for opportunities to experiment with estimation in the classroom each day.

## Block by Block                                           BEGINNING

INDIVIDUAL

Give the child a supply of identical blocks. Ask him to guess and then measure how many blocks it will take to fill the distance from one spot to another, for example, from one end of the desk to the other, across the cover of a big book, from one side of the door jamb to the other, and so on. Be sure to talk about each guess in relation to the actual distance to help the child make more accurate guesses in the future. Vary this activity by using other objects (drinking straws, paper clips, erasers, base 10 rods, etc.).

## Measure and Compare                                      BEGINNING

INDIVIDUAL

Give the child any measurement tool (blocks, drinking straws, paper clips, erasers, base 10 rods, etc.) and have her measure a short distance in the room, such as the distance from one side of a table to the other. Now pose a distance question, such as "Is the distance from the door to the rug longer or shorter than the distance measured on the table?" Have the child determine the answer using one of the measurement tools. Repeat with a different distance and another question.

# Babies and Giants

**INDIVIDUAL OR SMALL GROUP**

DEVELOPING

Show the children how to take baby steps and giant steps. Then ask them to choose two classroom objects they want to measure the distance between, like the chalkboard and your desk. Have them take the first measurement using baby steps and then ask them how many it took. Have them measure again in giant steps and ask how many. Discuss the reason for the differences in the results. Repeat with two other distances, but have the children estimate the number of baby steps and the number of giant steps before they measure.

# Miles to Go

**INDIVIDUAL OR SMALL GROUP**

DEVELOPING

Use masking tape to make 10 parallel lines about 6 inches apart on the floor, each measuring about 2 feet long. Number them from 1 to 10. Give the children toy cars (or paper cutouts of cars), making sure each child's cars are all the same size. Ask the children to estimate how many cars it will take to go from the first to the third line. Then have them find the actual answer by placing their cars end to end. Point out that the number of cars it will take depends on the size of the cars being used to measure the distance. Repeat the activity with other distances.

# Taking a Tour

**INDIVIDUAL, SMALL GROUP, OR WHOLE GROUP**

DEVELOPING

Take the children for a walk around the school and at various places have everyone stop. Ask them to estimate how many steps it will take to get from where they are standing to the fire extinguisher, for example, or to the next classroom doorway. Count steps as you all move to the specified location to check their estimates. Repeat with other destinations, and ask the children each time to think about how far the last distance was, and whether the next one will be shorter or longer, adjusting their estimates accordingly.

# Guess and Step

**DEVELOPING**

INDIVIDUAL OR SMALL GROUP

Write "____ steps" on several index cards and fill in each blank with a number from 1 to 15. You do not need to make one card for every number, but make sure to have an assortment of small and large numbers. Ask each child to draw a card and read its number. Then tell them to pick out something in the room that they estimate they could walk to, from where they are, in the number of steps specified on the card. For example, if a card reads "6 steps," the child will choose something he thinks is about six steps away. Have him walk to his chosen destination, counting each step, and then compare the actual number of steps to that on his card. Discuss the results and then have the children repeat the activity with new cards.

# Throw and Guess

**DEVELOPING/PROFICIENT**

INDIVIDUAL OR SMALL GROUP

Bring the children to an outside space or into a hallway. Show them how to carefully throw a beanbag underhand, guess the distance in steps, and then count the steps it takes you to get to where the beanbag landed. Give each child his own beanbag. Ask him to throw it, guess the distance in steps, and then count the actual number of steps. Mark his starting spot as well as landing spot with a piece of tape and ask him to throw the beanbag again. This time, before he makes his estimate, talk about where this toss landed in relation to the first toss. If it's closer, would it take more steps or fewer steps? What if it's farther away? Repeat the process with less discussion as estimates become more accurate.

# **Skill:** Combines objects (beanbags, marbles, beads, etc.) to make a greater number.

Asking a child to combine objects attaches a concrete representation to the concept of making more (later you'll use the word addition, of course). A child will quickly see that combining two sets of anything makes one larger set. When learning to identify the number of objects in a set, the child will eventually be able to recognize that counting doesn't always have to start with the number 1. The following activities will help children learn to count on, as well as combine groups.

## Target Totals

INDIVIDUAL

BEGINNING

Draw a bull's-eye target with three concentric circles on the ground or create one with tape on the floor. In the inner circle write the number 3, in the middle circle the number 2, and in the outer circle the number 1. Give the child two beanbags and a small supply of blocks. Have him stand two feet away from the target and toss a beanbag onto it two times. If his beanbags landed on the 2 and the 1, for example, he would take 2 blocks and then 1 block from his supply and describe the total number of blocks he has (3). Repeat another time or two. As his skill develops, experiment with a bigger target, a greater throwing distance, and different numbers.

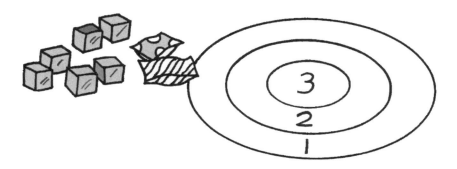

# Cube Connections

**BEGINNING**

INDIVIDUAL OR SMALL GROUP

Provide the children with a supply of Unifix cubes or something similar, making sure there are several different colors represented. Pose simple number stories such as "three red cubes were playing in the park. Four blue cubes asked if they could play too. The red cubes said yes. How many cubes are playing in the park now?" Have the children use the cubes to determine the answer, linking the two number sets together if desired.

# Follow the Recipe

**BEGINNING**

INDIVIDUAL OR SMALL GROUP

Check with parents or the school nurse regarding any food allergies before doing this activity. Gather together some small snack items (fish-shaped crackers, round crackers, pretzel sticks, cereal pieces, raisins, etc.). Place 10 of each food item on a paper plate and give that plate plus an empty plate to each child. Tell the children you are going to give them directions for making a snack. For example, you might say, "Take three fish crackers and two round crackers." The children count out the ingredients and then place them on their empty plates. Now ask them how many crackers they have in all. Repeat with the other food items, using different number combinations until you've included all of the ingredients.

# Jingle Bells in a Jar

**DEVELOPING**

INDIVIDUAL OR SMALL GROUP

Give each child a clean, plastic mayonnaise jar and 10 jingle bells. Tell the children to place a specific number of bells, between 1 and 10, into their jars, for example, 6. Next, ask them how many bells would be in their jars if they added 3 more. Encourage the children to count on from the number of bells already in their jars to determine the total. Model this by touching the jar and saying, "Six; now count the other 3 you want to add: 7, 8, 9." Eventually the children should be able to count the additional bells without touching each one.

# Joker's Wild

DEVELOPING

INDIVIDUAL

Give the child a stack of playing cards, each with a value of five or less. Ask him to draw two cards from his deck, turn them over, and point to the number that's larger. Then have him tell you how many of the larger hearts, clubs, diamonds, or spades are on both cards together (to distinguish from the smaller ones that are next to the numbers on the cards). Encourage him to start with the larger number and count on from there if he's ready. If not, counting all of the large hearts, etc., is acceptable.

# Fast Fingers

DEVELOPING/PROFICIENT

INDIVIDUAL, SMALL GROUP (in pairs),
OR WHOLE GROUP (in pairs)

Both you and the child, or each pair of children, stand or sit with your hands behind your back. Explain that on a count of three, each person in the pair will bring one hand forward showing any number of fingers they wish. In turn, each child starts with the number of fingers she held up, adds on the number of fingers her partner held up, and determines the total number of fingers. Practice having the children name the total as quickly as possible.

# Counting Frame Combos

DEVELOPING/PROFICIENT

INDIVIDUAL

Give the child an abacus or a counting frame and have her show you one to five beads on the first row of the abacus. Then tell her to add one to five more to that group. Ask her how many beads there are now in that row in all. Play with adding on and taking away within the row of 10 beads. For example, you might say, "Show me six beads. Take away two beads. How many are there now?"

# Skill: Counts objects aloud with accuracy (to 100).

When practicing this skill, children will likely use a variety of strategies to count. It is okay for them to count each object individually, by 2s, 5s, or another way. The goal here is accuracy, not speed, so create a relaxed atmosphere and begin with smaller numbers. As a child's skill in counting aloud increases, include larger numbers in the activities you choose.

## Bagging Groceries

BEGINNING

INDIVIDUAL

Gather some paper grocery bags and a collection of artificial food items or small, empty food containers (yogurt cups, individual-serving cereal boxes, juice boxes, etc.). Ask the child to place a specified number of items into a bag, counting the objects out loud as she does so. Begin with just a few items and then increase the number as the child becomes more skilled.

## Magic Wand

BEGINNING

INDIVIDUAL OR
SMALL GROUP

Supply each child with a magnetic wand (like the ones used for science experiments) and a pile of metal-rimmed plastic chips (paper clips will also work). Ask the children to wave their magic wands over the pile once, and then count out loud as they remove each chip from the magnetic force of their wands. The children can place the chips back into the original pile or form separate piles each time they remove the attached chips, and then count the sum of all the piles.

Number Facts & Jumping Jacks

# Grab Bag

INDIVIDUAL

BEGINNING/DEVELOPING

Give the child a resealable plastic bag full of small objects such as plastic beads or buttons. Ask him to reach into the bag, take out a handful, and count them out loud. As he becomes more skilled, he can reach in with his other hand, take another handful, and continue counting from the number he ended on when counting the first handful. For those children who are not yet secure with counting to higher numbers, place larger objects in the bag so they are not able to grab as many at one time.

# Eggs in a Basket

INDIVIDUAL

BEGINNING/DEVELOPING

Supply the child with a tote bag of plastic eggs, and place three or four baskets in a line on the floor. As the child comes to each basket, ask her to place a certain number of eggs in it, counting them aloud as she does so. She may choose to place one egg in the basket at a time, attempt to place two in at a time (one in each hand), or use another strategy. Exploration of counting strategies is excellent, but be sure she maintains accuracy when doing this. As a variation, use socks and laundry baskets if you have enough space.

# Pennies in the Piggy

INDIVIDUAL

DEVELOPING

Gather several small, resealable plastic bags, 100 pennies, and a piggy bank. (You can use a real bank or make one from a plastic mayonnaise jar, a shoe box, or a milk carton with a slot cut in the top.) Place a different number of pennies in each bag. Ask the child to choose a bag and count the pennies out loud as she drops them into the bank. When she's finished with one bag, she can select another and start counting from one again, or continue counting from where she left off with the previous bag.

# You Can Count on It

INDIVIDUAL

PROFICIENT

Place an abacus on a table or desk in front of the child. Move a small number of beads together and ask her to count them aloud. If she is correct, congratulate her and push all the beads back to their starting point. Move another set of beads together and repeat this process. Celebrate when she begins to recognize groups of 10 and then counts on to determine the complete number value. Practice for a maximum of 5 to 10 minutes, ensuring that the child experiences success and has fun.

# Birds on a Wire

INDIVIDUAL

PROFICIENT

Create pictures on your computer of birds lined up in rows, similar to the way beads are arranged on an abacus. Put 10 birds in each row. Print out several sets of 10, laminate them, and cut some into individual birds. Give the child some sets with 10 birds and some single birds. Pick a number such as 13, which would be shown as one row with 10 birds and one row with 3. Ask him to count the number of birds shown aloud. Since most children will count every bird at first, it is best to begin this activity with a small number. As the child learns to recognize and count by groups of 10, increase the values used for this exercise. Experiment with patterns of number values, such as 12, 22, 32.

# Skill: Understands concepts of add on and take away (using manipulatives).

While they are developing this skill, children are also building their understanding of math vocabulary and the cause and effect of mathematical processes. Using manipulatives such as counters, cubes, and chips allows children to explore math in a concrete way. This will ease their path to understanding the abstract numerical representations they will encounter as they continue in school.

## Pigs in the Puddle          BEGINNING

INDIVIDUAL OR SMALL GROUP

Cut a mud puddle shape out of a brown paper bag or a piece of brown paper. Make 10 paper pigs or use small plastic ones. Sit across from the children, place three of the pigs in the puddle, and tell them there are three pigs in the puddle. Add two more pigs and ask the children if there are more than three pigs or fewer than three pigs in the puddle. Then ask how they know without counting. Add pigs a few more times, asking children how the number has changed, and then start taking them away.

## More and Less          BEGINNING

INDIVIDUAL OR SMALL GROUP

Supply each child with a pile of small wooden blocks. Ask what would need to happen in order for there to be fewer blocks in their respective piles. (Each child would need to take some blocks out of the pile.) Ask them to show you fewer blocks. Have each child take the blocks they removed from the pile and place them away from the original pile. Now have a similar conversation about showing more. How would they make the pile have more in it than it does right now? (Each child would need to add some of the blocks taken out.) Ask them to show you more. You can repeat the activity by asking them to show you "a lot less" or "a lot more" and asking questions such as: If we added just one, would it still be more than it was? Such comparisons, conversations, and mathematical terms are invaluable.

# Laundry Day

INDIVIDUAL

BEGINNING

Make some paper cutouts in the shape of T-shirts. On your work table, tape a piece of yarn or string to resemble a clothesline. Place 10 shirts in a basket (the clothes basket). Start the activity by "hanging" two to five shirts on the clothesline. Ask the child to identify how many shirts are on the line. Then have him identify how many shirts are still in the basket. Now pose different add-on and take-away tasks for him to complete. Add two more shirts to the line and ask him, "Are there more shirts on the line? Are there more in the basket? How many are on the line? How many are in the basket?" Allow recounting if necessary at this stage.

# Cube-It

INDIVIDUAL

DEVELOPING

Link 10 Unifix cubes together and place them on the table in front of the child, telling him there are 10 cubes in the set. Give him 9 unlinked cubes; tell him to connect them and to place the set of 9 below the set of 10. Ask him to identify how many cubes are in his set without counting each one (9). The goal is that he will be able to use his knowledge of the original 10 cubes to help identify the number in his set. Ask him to add a cube to his set and to identify how many there are now. Continue with add-on tasks and include some take-away tasks with 1 to 3 cubes. Each time, allow the child to use the original set of 10 to help determine how many are in his new set.

# Stringing Beads

**INDIVIDUAL**

DEVELOPING

Supply the child with 10 large beads and a long pipe cleaner with a knot on the end. Ask her to string the beads and tell you how many there are. Then ask her to take two away and tell you how many are left on the pipe cleaner. Encourage her to identify the number without relying on counting every bead every time. Continue to pose add-on and take-away tasks with one to three beads. If necessary, you can start with fewer than 10 beads and work your way up as the child becomes more skilled.

# From Zero to Six(ty)

**INDIVIDUAL OR SMALL GROUP**

DEVELOPING/PROFICIENT

Give each child 3 beads strung onto a pipe cleaner with a knot in one end. Place a pile of additional beads within reach, and a die with its sides programmed as follows: +1, +2, +3, -1, -2, -3. In turn, each child rolls the die and adds on or takes away beads according to what was rolled. If it was +2, then the child adds 2 beads to the pipe cleaner and identifies how many are now on it (5). When he rolls again, he follows the directive on the die and describes the number of beads now on the pipe cleaner. While accuracy is obviously important, you also want each child to be able to manipulate and identify the number of beads quickly.

# Aba-Count

**INDIVIDUAL**

DEVELOPING/PROFICIENT

Give the child an abacus. Move two to five beads together and ask her to count the number of beads you moved and tell you how many there are. Ask her to take away a specific number of beads from this group and to identify the result. If there were five beads and you asked her to move (take away) three, there would be two left. Repeat with an add-on task. Alternate between adding on and taking away, encouraging the child to recognize quickly how many are shown each time. At this point in the development of this skill, you need not always start with the same number of beads. Whatever number was left from the previous task can be the starting point for the next task.

# Skill: Recognizes number groups to 10 without counting every object.

A child's ability to recognize small number groups without having to count each object will help her to be successful with more complicated mathematical transactions later. Developing this skill builds acumen and confidence, plus automaticity with mental math problems, estimation skills, and a deeper understanding of number relationships.

## Start Out Slowly

INDIVIDUAL

BEGINNING

Use counting bears or something similar for this activity. Sit down opposite the child at a table or desk. Place one, two, or three bears in front of the child and ask her to tell you how many there are without counting each one. Continue to show her one, two, or three bears randomly until she can identify consistently the number of bears *without* counting.

## Finger Flash

INDIVIDUAL

BEGINNING

Have the child sit facing you. Starting with one hand, show him a certain number of fingers for five seconds. Put your hand down and ask him to show you quickly the same number of fingers you showed him. Continue with other finger flashes on one hand (1 to 5), adding the other hand (6 to 10) as he becomes more skilled. If he's not successful at first, show him fewer fingers or show them for a longer period of time, and let him count them if necessary. As his skill improves, display your fingers for shorter times, eventually flashing them for a second only.

# Spin a High Five

## INDIVIDUAL OR SMALL GROUP (in pairs)

BEGINNING/DEVELOPING

Make a game spinner containing eight sections. In each section, attach one to five stickers, repeating the number of stickers as desired. In turn, have each child spin the spinner and identify the number of stickers on the section where the spinner stops. Tell her to do this quickly without counting each one. Have the player who did not spin verify the number of stickers, counting them if necessary, and high five the spinner if she was correct. Be sure to keep track of how many correct guesses each child makes out of the total number of times she spins.

# Lots of Dots

## INDIVIDUAL OR SMALL GROUP

BEGINNING/DEVELOPING

Place a set of double-six dominoes in an opaque bag. Have one of the children take out a domino and identify the number of dots on one end and then on the other end. If she is correct, she keeps the domino; if not, she places it back in the bag. Next, another player takes a turn. As the children's skills increase, add dominoes that have up to double nines and encourage them to identify the number groups without counting every dot.

# Swatting Flies

## INDIVIDUAL

DEVELOPING

Attach pieces of Velcro to a brand-new flyswatter. Pile 10 or 12 black pompoms (flies) on a desk or table and give the child the flyswatter. Tell him to swat the pile of "flies" and quickly try to identify how many he struck, without counting if possible, by looking at the number group on the swatter. After he names the number, he removes the pompoms, places them back in the pile, and swats some more.

# Peek-a-Boo

**INDIVIDUAL**

DEVELOPING

Bring a tray and 10 crayons (or 10 of another manipulative) to the table. Ask the child to cover his eyes or turn around while you place a certain number of crayons on the tray. Tell him that when you say "peek-a-boo," he will turn around for five seconds and try to identify the number group you've represented on the tray. Allow him to check his guess by counting the crayons. Repeat the process, varying the number of crayons each time.

# Lily Pads

**INDIVIDUAL OR SMALL GROUP**

DEVELOPING

On a large sheet of blue bulletin board paper (the pond), paste 10 green paper lily pads, each containing a different number of paper frogs or frog stickers, ranging from 1 to 10. Give each child a beanbag and have one child toss her beanbag into the pond. Ask her to name the number group (represented by the frogs) that the beanbag landed on or near. Verify her response and then repeat the procedure with the next player.

# Now You See Them

**INDIVIDUAL**

DEVELOPING/PROFICIENT

Gather a collection of 10 pompoms and a piece of tagboard measuring about 9 x 12 inches. Sit at a table facing the child. Hold up the tagboard between you and the child so he cannot see the pompoms. Arrange a group of two or three pompoms, lift up the tagboard for a count of three to five seconds, and then replace the barrier. Ask the child to tell you how many pompoms were in the group. Repeat with other number groups up to 10. If the child is not successful, decrease the number of pompoms you use, since you want his success rate to be high.

# Abacus Counting

DEVELOPING/PROFICIENT

INDIVIDUAL

Place an abacus in front of the child and position the beads so they are all pushed over to the same side. Tell the child that you want him to focus only on the first row of beads for each round of this exercise. Next, move a certain number of beads over to the other side and ask the child to tell you (without counting the individual beads) how many are in the group you moved. Show him random groups of 1 to 10 beads, each time giving him only three to five seconds to identify the number group. As a variation, you can hold up a piece of tagboard between the child and the abacus so you can change the number group, show it to him briefly, and then cover it up again.

**Skill:** Shows groups of objects to correctly represent numbers to 10.

Part of becoming a successful mathematician is recognizing the relationships between numbers. The following exercises help children learn to quickly demonstrate the value of a number and to see and feel how much smaller or larger a number is compared to other familiar numbers.

## Draw and Draw

BEGINNING

INDIVIDUAL OR
SMALL GROUP

Give the child a small dry-erase board, a nonpermanent marker, a sock for an eraser, and a pile of index cards, each with a numeral from 1 to 10 written on it. Ask her to pick one card, identify the number, and draw that number of stars, squares, dots, circles, or other shapes on her board. When you've checked her drawing for accuracy, have her erase the board, draw another card, and repeat the procedure.

## Pickup Sticks

BEGINNING

INDIVIDUAL

Place a pile of Pickup or Popsicle sticks in front of the child on a table or on the floor. Ask him to pick up a number you specify (from 1 to 10) and to show you that group of sticks as quickly as possible. Tell him not to worry about the rules of the traditional game of Pickup Sticks. The goal here is to show you quickly specific number groups.

# Bowling for Numbers

**INDIVIDUAL**

DEVELOPING

Gather 10 plastic bowling pins or empty two-liter soda bottles and a playground ball. Tell the child to set up a specific number of pins (from 1 to 10). After you've checked his counting, allow him to bowl to see how many pins he can knock down just for fun. Have him set up another specified number of pins, check his counting, and let him bowl again.

# Inside Out

**INDIVIDUAL**

DEVELOPING

Place a hula hoop at one end of your work space. Have the child stand a few feet away from it, depending on her throwing accuracy, and give her a container with 10 beanbags. Tell her to toss a certain number of beanbags into the hoop and to stop when she's reached that number. (Beanbags that fall outside the hoop are not counted.) Check her accuracy, have her collect the beanbags, and repeat the activity.

# Dealer's Choice

**INDIVIDUAL**

DEVELOPING

Write a different number from 1 to 10 on index cards. Arrange four of the cards in a semicircle in front of the child and tell her they are the "players." Give her a deck of traditional playing cards and tell her to deal to each player the same number of cards as indicated on the player's face (that is, the number you wrote on the index card). Once you've checked her accuracy, replace the players with four new index cards with different numbers on them, and have her repeat the process.

# Fast Figuring

**DEVELOPING/PROFICIENT**

INDIVIDUAL

Give the child a small pile of interlocking cubes. Ask him to link together a number that you specify (from 1 to 10) as quickly as possible. Then give him another number from 1 to 10 and tell him to either add it to or take it away from the cubes he has already linked. Encourage him to show you the resulting set of linked cubes as quickly as possible, with the goal being 10 seconds or less.

# Absolutely Abacus I

**DEVELOPING/PROFICIENT**

INDIVIDUAL

Give the child an abacus or counting frame and tell her to show you the number that you specify (from 1 to 10) as quickly as she can. Start with smaller numbers so that she is successful right away. Gradually work up to larger ones until she can show the numbers quickly and without having to count the individual beads.

**Skill:** Adds on or takes away from a group (to 10).

Some of the activities for the skill "Understands concepts of add on and take away (using manipulatives)" on pages 53–55 will work here as well. Simply increase the number of objects the children are adding on or taking away to include numbers up to 10. The goal here is to encourage the child to recognize the new number quickly and without counting each individual object. Remember that a high rate of success is important, so you may need to start with one to three objects at first and build from there as the child becomes more adept at doing the mental math.

## Little Bo Peep                                       BEGINNING

INDIVIDUAL, SMALL GROUP, OR WHOLE GROUP

Create a "pasture" from a piece of green paper and use cotton balls for sheep or cut them out of white paper. Give a pasture and five sheep to each child. Tell the children to put all five sheep in the pasture and then pose simple tasks, such as, "Take away three sheep. How many are in the pasture now?" Let sheep wander in and out of the pasture in increasing numbers as the children become more able to identify small additions and subtractions quickly and consistently.

## Sticky Note Parade                                   BEGINNING

INDIVIDUAL

On a tabletop or your white board, mark off a rectangular work space for the child. To one side of this, place a number of sticky notes (any shape and size). Tell the child to put a specified number of sticky notes in her work space, and then pose add-on or take-away tasks. For example, you might tell her to add four more sticky notes to her work space and identify the resulting number, take away three and say the number, add on five, and so forth. Each time she sticks or unsticks notes to her work space, she creates a new number that you want her to identify quickly.

# Eraser Race

**INDIVIDUAL OR SMALL GROUP**

DEVELOPING

Provide the child with a nonpermanent marker, a sock for an eraser, and a dry-erase board. (He can use a small one in his lap or stand at one mounted on the wall.) Tell the child to mark a specific number of short vertical lines on his board, for example, six. Then tell him to erase, or take away, five of the lines and to identify the new number. Next, tell him to add on seven and again identify the number. Continue in a quick manner, encouraging mental math as opposed to allowing time for him to count each vertical line.

# Counting Cookies

**INDIVIDUAL**

DEVELOPING

Create 10 cookie-shaped paper cutouts. (If desired, attach a small piece of magnetic tape to the back of each one.) Place the "cookies" onto an old cookie sheet. Using numbers up to 10 and in random order, tell the child to add on or take away a specific number of cookies from the sheet. Each time she performs a task have her identify the resulting number of cookies.

# Traffic Jam

**INDIVIDUAL, SMALL GROUP, OR WHOLE GROUP**

DEVELOPING

Make a road by cutting black construction paper in a wavy shape. Give the paper road and 10 toy cars to each child. Ask them to place a specified number of cars on the road. Then tell them to add on a certain number more and to identify how many cars are in the traffic jam. Have them add or take away cars at your direction. Each time cars move, ask them to give you a traffic update as to how many cars are now on the road.

# Back and Forth

INDIVIDUAL

DEVELOPING/PROFICIENT

Give the child an abacus and ask her to concentrate on just the first row of 10 beads. Tell her to move a specified number of beads over to one side. Then have her add on or take away beads from this group and quickly identify the resulting number. Have fun with this task for two or three minutes.

# Skill: Recognizes number groups to 100 without counting every object.

As children's numeracy skills become more developed, they should be able to recognize number groups without having to count every object within the group. The best way to encourage growth in this area is to work with groups of 10, adding single items to the 10s as the child becomes more skilled. While accuracy is important, you should also be looking for automaticity at this point, so time is another factor to consider in determining proficiency.

## Rainbow Rows                                              BEGINNING

**INDIVIDUAL OR SMALL GROUP**

Use a set of blank 10 x 10 grids and different colors to demonstrate a variety of number values. For example, you might use red on one grid to color the first full row of 10 boxes and 4 boxes in the next row (14). On another grid, use blue to color 3 full rows plus 6 on the next row (36). Use green on a third grid and color 4 full rows (40). Prepare 5 to 10 number grids and use them like flash cards, asking each child in turn to identify what number each colored set of boxes indicates. As the children become successful at identifying these number values, replace a couple of the familiar number grids with new ones showing different number values. Maintain a high success rate by adjusting tasks based on each child's responses.

## Cut-Ups                                              BEGINNING/DEVELOPING

**INDIVIDUAL OR SMALL GROUP**

Laminate some blank 10 x 10 grids. Cut the grids into pieces that represent different numbers, being sure to maintain complete rows of 10 as well as some partial rows. For example, a cut-up that showed 58 would be 5 complete rows of 10 and 8 boxes in the next row of 10. Ask the children to tell you the number value represented without counting every box.

# At the Movies

**INDIVIDUAL**

DEVELOPING

Prepare 10 rows of smiley face stickers on paper strips, 10 stickers per strip. Cut one strip apart so you have some "ones," or single faces. Tell the child that the faces represent people in a movie theatre. Each time you show her a group of faces, she will tell you how many people are watching the movie. Before you display a number, have her turn around in her chair or cover her eyes. Then have her look at the display of strips and tell you quickly, without counting every face, how many people are at the movies. She should be counting each full row by 10s and then counting on for the additional single faces.

# Counting with Cubes

**INDIVIDUAL**

DEVELOPING

Connect Unifix cubes into 10 rows of 10 cubes each. Sit at a table facing the child and place a file folder, standing on end, as a screen between you. Create any number up to 100 with the cubes. For example, you would make the number 27 by showing 2 rows of 10 and 7 additional cubes linked in the third row. Remove the file folder and ask the child to identify the number of cubes you've shown as quickly as she can and without counting every cube. Replace the file folder screen, rearrange the cubes to show another number, and repeat the process, using larger numbers as her accuracy and speed increase.

# Base 10 Rides Again

**INDIVIDUAL OR SMALL GROUP**

DEVELOPING

With a collection of base 10 blocks, sit facing the child at a table. Show any number up to 100 with the blocks and ask him to identify the number you made as quickly as he can. Begin with smaller numbers or rods only to show round numbers like 20, 40, or 70. When he is successful with these, start including one or two single blocks with the rods of 10 so he is recognizing numbers like 32 or 81. Continue adding individual blocks to show numbers like 69 or 78.

# Count in a Flash

DEVELOPING/PROFICIENT

INDIVIDUAL

Sit at a table opposite the child with an abacus between you. Display a number up to 100 with the beads and give the child five seconds to identify the value. If she is not successful in five seconds, use easier values for the next round. Play with number patterns, like 12, 22, 32, and 52, to help the child learn base 10 relationships. Allow lots of time to practice this activity. Deep understanding of this skill is essential for long-term math success.

# Skill: Shows groups of objects by number (to 100).

Showing numbers to 100 reveals the child's ability to deeply understand number patterns, number sets, number relationships, and number complements. To ensure success, start with numbers below 30. Allow the child to make comments or observations about the work he is doing. These conversations will enrich his understanding. As the child becomes more skilled, encourage him to take the quickest route to displaying the correct number. Try not to show him shortcuts—let the child figure out the patterns and shortcuts on his own.

## Absolutely Abacus II

INDIVIDUAL

BEGINNING

Give the child an abacus or counting frame and ask her to quickly show you a specified number from 1 to 10. Gradually increase the range until she can accurately and quickly show any number from 1 to 30 without needing to count individual beads.

## Count and Connect I

INDIVIDUAL OR SMALL GROUP

BEGINNING

Connect 30 Unifix cubes into three groups of 10, placing each group of 10 under another in parallel lines. Make a set of 30 for each child in the group. Ask the children to use the cubes to show you numbers between 1 and 30, taking apart groups of 10 as needed. Allow them enough time to display the number you specify but encourage them to avoid counting every cube.

NUMERACY SKILLS

# Abacus Patterns

**INDIVIDUAL**

DEVELOPING

Give the child an abacus or counting frame and ask her to quickly show you any number up to 30, for example, 22. Then ask her to add on groups of 10 to this number. Let her figure out on her own how the pattern of 22, 32, 42, 52, etc. works. Play with this concept by choosing a starting number and asking the child to add or subtract groups of 10, 20, or 30.

# Blocks and Cards

**INDIVIDUAL, SMALL GROUP, OR WHOLE GROUP**

DEVELOPING

Supply each child with a collection of base 10 blocks consisting of 9 rods and 10 cubes, plus a stack of traditional playing cards with the face cards removed. For each round, have him draw two cards from the deck and then create the two 2-digit numbers possible with the base 10 blocks. For example, if the child drew a 5 and a 7, he would show you 57 and then 75 with the blocks. When he has done this successfully, he discards the two playing cards, draws two more, and repeats the process. If you are doing this with your entire class, circulate to check the children's work as they are ready, reminding them to leave the cards out so you can see what numbers they were supposed to make.

# Framed

**INDIVIDUAL**

DEVELOPING

Create 10 laminated 10-frames (5 x 2 grids of 10 colored boxes) on separate pieces of paper. Supply the child with all the frames and some round counters like bingo chips or pennies. Have the child show you different numbers between 1 and 100 using the frames and the counters. For example, if you asked her to show 82, she would display 8 of the 10-frames plus 2 of the bingo chips. For 55, she would display 5 of the 10-frames and 5 of the bingo chips.

# Count and Connect II

DEVELOPING/PROFICIENT

INDIVIDUAL

Connect 100 Unifix cubes into 10 groups of 10, placing each group under another in parallel lines so they resemble the beads on an abacus. Tell the child to use the cubes to show the number you specify (up to 100), pulling apart connected groups of 10 as needed.

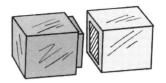

Start with small numbers and gradually increase the difficulty. Allow him up to 10 seconds to display each number but encourage him to avoid counting each individual cube.

# Absolutely Abacus III

DEVELOPING/PROFICIENT

INDIVIDUAL

Give the child an abacus or counting frame and ask her to quickly show you a number you specify (from 1 to 100) without counting individual beads. Take time to practice this skill to mastery and automaticity. As a variation, add two dice to the activity, one with the numbers 1 to 6 on it and the other with the numbers 4 to 9. For each round, have the child roll the dice, identify both of the two-digit numbers that can be made with the dice, and choose one to display on the abacus. For example, if she rolled 2 and 5, she could select 25 or 52. As her skill increases, encourage her to display the number as quickly as she can, with 10 seconds or less being the ultimate goal.

> **Skill:** Adds on or takes away from a group (to 100).
>
> Giving children practice visualizing numbers of things up to 100 will ultimately prepare them for most of the other mathematical thinking they will do in their lives (following a recipe, figuring a tip, making a budget, etc.). We want children to be more comfortable with mathematical principles than many adults are. By developing this skill, you will also help them build number pattern awareness, mental math ability, estimation skills, and math fact automaticity.

# Round and Round We Go                                   BEGINNING

INDIVIDUAL OR SMALL GROUP

Place an abacus on a table in front of each child. Ask them to show you a certain round number, for example, 30. Then tell them to add on another round number, such as 40, and identify the resulting number. Next, have them take away another round number, such as 20, and again identify the number. Repeat as time allows. Having the children work with groups of 10 will build confidence and keep their success rates high.

# Color Me                                    BEGINNING/DEVELOPING

INDIVIDUAL OR SMALL GROUP

Supply each child with a blank, laminated 10 x 10 grid, a dry-erase marker, and an old sock to use as an eraser. Begin by asking each child to show you a particular number by drawing lines through or quickly coloring in the boxes. So if you said 46, they would mark through the first four full rows and six boxes in the next row. Tell them to add on another number, which you specify, by marking through additional boxes, and then have them identify the new number shown. To take away a number, they erase the number of boxes you specify and then identify the resulting number.

# Flipping Out

**INDIVIDUAL**                                                              DEVELOPING

Write any number from 1 to 100 on each of 20 index cards. Place the stack of cards (blank side up) on a table next to the child. Give the child an abacus, identify a starting number, and tell him to display it. Next, have him flip over an index card and identify the number on it, and then tell him to either add on or take away the number on the card from the starting number displayed on the abacus. Ask him to show it on the abacus first and then identify the new number. You may want to start with cards that have single-digit numbers and, as the child becomes more skilled, move on to 10s or multiples of 5, and then to more challenging numbers.

# Number Spies

**INDIVIDUAL OR SMALL GROUP**                                               DEVELOPING

Give each child an abacus and pose different add-on or take-away tasks. Start them out with any number you wish and then use the refrain: "I spy with my little eye a number that is ___ less/more. Can you 'spy' that number too? Show me." Each child completes the add-on or take-away instruction and tells you the number of beads she spies after each action.

# Roll of the Dice

**INDIVIDUAL**                                                              DEVELOPING

Connect Unifix cubes so that you have 10 rows of 10 cubes each. Using a single die, cover the sides with masking tape and write a number from 4 to 9 on each of the sides. Do the same with another die but use the numbers 1 to 6. Give the child the connected cubes and the die showing numbers 4 to 9. Ask her to show you a number you specify (up to 100) with the cubes. Then have her roll the die, add on or take away the number shown on it, and tell you what the new number is. Once she is successful using single-digit numbers, give her the other die and have her roll both. Then tell her to add on or take away one of the numbers created by the two digits on the dice. For example, if she rolled a 4 and a 5, she could use 45 or 54. Have her tell you the number created after adding on or taking away the two-digit number.

# Where Are You?

INDIVIDUAL

DEVELOPING/PROFICIENT

Give the child a blank 10 x 10 grid and a bingo chip or penny. Tell him to find the box for a specific number, 53 for example, and to mark it on the grid with his chip (he should have moved down five full rows of 10 and then counted three boxes into the next row). Ask him to take away 5, place his chip on that new number (48), and tell you what it is. Then have him add on 23 and identify that number (71), and so on. Continue with both add on and take away tasks that involve any number up to 100.

# Abacus Antics

DEVELOPING/PROFICIENT

Sit opposite the child at a table and place an abacus between the two of you. Tell her a number story with elements that will require her to add at times and to take away at other times, using the beads on the abacus. After each of these elements, have her tell you how many beads the abacus is showing. A story might be as follows: 36 ants left the hill (have her show you 36 beads) on their way to a picnic. A few minutes later, 14 more ants joined them (she adds on 14). How many ants are there now? (She shows 50.) About halfway there, 22 of the ants got tired and went back to their hill. How many ants are there now? (28) Continue telling the story with other numbers up to 100 or create a new story using larger numbers when the child is ready.

**Skill:** Identifies place values (ones, tens, hundreds, thousands).

Identifying place value is a complex skill. Children need to know "physically" where a digit is within the number and what that place is called. They also need to be able to determine the **value** of a digit within a number (in 67, the 6 has a value of 60). Start with two-digit numbers since most children are familiar with these. Increase to three- and four-digit numbers only when a child's success rate shows he is ready for the challenge.

## Popsicle Stick Place Value                               BEGINNING

INDIVIDUAL OR SMALL GROUP

You will need a set of 10 sticks for every child. Write a number from 0 to 9 on one end of each Popsicle stick or tongue depressor, making sure each has a different number. Place each set of 10 sticks in a separate cup and give a cup to every child. The children draw two sticks out of their cups and lay them on the table side by side. In turn, ask each one to tell you what number the two digits created, what *place* each number is in, and what the *value* of each number is in that place. Next, have the children reverse the order of their sticks, and ask the same questions. Then have them replace the sticks, draw two more, and repeat the process.

## Rollin' to 100                               BEGINNING

INDIVIDUAL

Supply the child with a laminated 100 chart, a die, and a bingo chip or penny. Tell her to place her chip on the grid on the number one. Have her roll the die and move her chip that number of spaces on the grid, tell you what number she landed on, and then give you the place and value of each digit of the number. If you want her to work on three-digit numbers, simply create a grid that goes from 101 to 200, for example, and repeat the same procedure.

# Face Up Match

**INDIVIDUAL, SMALL GROUP, OR WHOLE GROUP**

BEGINNING

Write a different two-digit number on each of five index cards and underline one of the digits. On five other cards, write the place and the value of each of the underlined numbers. So one card might read "4<u>6</u>" and its match would read "10s place, 40." Make a set of cards for each child in the group; the sets need not be identical. Have the children arrange them face up in two columns on a table, desk, or floor. The column on the left should have all of the number cards and the column on the right should have the cards with the values. Tell them to match a card in the left column with a card in the right column placing them side by side. After you've checked their work, children can exchange cards with a classmate and repeat the process.

# Where Are You Now?

**INDIVIDUAL OR SMALL GROUP**

BEGINNING/DEVELOPING

Give each child a 100 chart and a bingo chip or penny. Tell him to place his chip on any number he wishes, and then tell you what the number is and what place and value each digit represents. Give directions such as, "Move your chip up two spaces. Where are you now?" He moves his chip, determines the number, and answers your questions about place and value. Continue with other directions, such as *down, to the left, to the right,* and *diagonally*.

# High Roller

**SMALL GROUP**

DEVELOPING

Give the group three or four number dice. Have a child roll the dice, create the largest number she can with the numbers rolled, and write it down. Ask the group to say the number aloud. The process continues as each child takes a turn rolling the dice and attempting to become "High Roller." Remind the group to say the number aloud each time before the next child rolls the dice.

# Highlighters

INDIVIDUAL, SMALL GROUP, OR WHOLE GROUP

DEVELOPING

Create a work sheet that has two columns and four boxes in each column. In each box, write a two-, three-, or four-digit number. Give each child a copy of the work sheet and a highlighter. Call out a number that appears on the sheet and ask the children to locate it. Once they have, tell them to highlight the numeral in the tens place or highlight the digit whose value is 20, and so forth. Repeat the process until all of the numbers have been called at least once.

# Mystery Numbers

INDIVIDUAL

DEVELOPING

Prepare a set of five or more index cards, each containing a two- or three-digit number. Place them in front of the child. Give her place value clues about one of the numbers and have her identify which one you're describing. For example, if one of the cards has the number 189, a clue might be "The mystery number has an 8 in the 10s place." Once the child identifies the correct number, have her tell you the value of the other digits.

# Show Me a Number

INDIVIDUAL, SMALL GROUP, OR WHOLE GROUP

DEVELOPING/PROFICIENT

Give each child a small dry-erase board, a nonpermanent marker, and an old sock for an eraser. For each round, ask the children to write on their dry-erase boards a number with a specified value or place. For example, you might ask them to show you a three-digit number that has an 80 in it. Children could write 489, 183, 685, and so forth. As the children show they are ready, increase the challenge by using four-digit numbers.

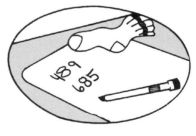

# Colorful Place Value

**DEVELOPING/PROFICIENT**

INDIVIDUAL OR SMALL GROUP

Create a work sheet that has two columns of three- and four-digit numbers in random order. Give each child a copy along with two different colored markers. Ask the children to circle all the numbers with values in the thousands with one color and all the numbers with values in the hundreds with the other color. When they have finished, pose questions about the values of the different numbers circled. For example, if one of the numbers is 1,406, you might ask, "What is the value of the 4?" (400). "What place is the 1 in? (the thousands place)."

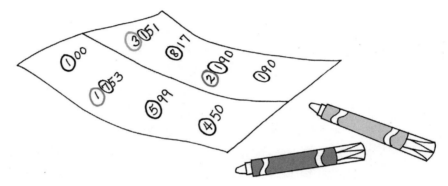

# Skill: Skip counts with manipulatives to a multiple of 10.

When a child is practicing skip counting, it is important for him to not only **say** the numbers but also **show** them. You want to move him past rote recitation to an understanding of the numerical patterns at work and visual representation of the objects being counted. Traditionally, skip counting practice begins with 10s, goes to 5s, and then 2s, with the other number patterns being introduced as the child gains a deeper understanding of them. A child should have a solid ability to skip count by any number from 2 to 10 before he is expected to memorize multiplication or division facts.

## A Show of Hands

BEGINNING

INDIVIDUAL

Create cutouts of hands that clearly show all five fingers and laminate them for repeated use. Make enough so that the child can display up to 100 fingers (20 hands). Tell the child to count by fives to any number up to 100. Tell her that as she counts, she must also show you the correct number of fingers for each number. So when she says "10," she should be showing you two hands.

## Connect and Count

BEGINNING

INDIVIDUAL

Supply the child with at least 50 Unifix cubes. Ask him to link the cubes together in sets of 2, 3, 4, or 5 and to skip count by that number to its multiple of 10, showing you the correct number of cubes each time he extends the count. So he would count by 3s to 30, by 4s to 40, and so forth.

# Picture Counting

**DEVELOPING**

INDIVIDUAL

Collect pictures of objects that have a specific number attached to them, like traffic lights (3), bicycle tires (2), cat's paws (4), spider legs (8), and so forth. Make copies of the pictures as needed to ensure that the child can count to the highest number you request. Give her a pile of pictures of traffic lights, for example, and ask her to use them to count by 3s to 30, showing the correct number of traffic lights each time she continues the count. Repeat with pictures of other objects and their corresponding skip counting pattern.

# It's All in the Beads

**DEVELOPING/PROFICIENT**

INDIVIDUAL

Give the child an abacus and ask her to use it to count by 2s, 5s, or 10s to a multiple of 10. Each time she extends the count, she displays the correct number of beads, using all those in one row before moving onto the next. Tell her that as she says each number in the sequence, she should also pay attention to how that number "looks" (or is represented) on the abacus. As her skill increases, have her use the abacus to count by more difficult sequences, for example, by 4s, 6s, or 8s.

# Count It Out

**DEVELOPING/PROFICIENT**

INDIVIDUAL

Give the child 10 dessert-size paper plates and a bag containing a counting manipulative of your choice, such as pennies. Tell him you want him to count by 7s to 70, for example. As he counts, he is to place 7 pennies on each plate as he says each number in the sequence out loud.

# Flash Card Abacus

DEVELOPING/PROFICIENT

INDIVIDUAL

Give the child an abacus and have a set of multiplication flash cards ready. Pick one card; let's say it reads 8 x 6 = 48. Ask the child to count by 8s or 6s to 48 on the abacus. Each time she extends the count, she displays that number of beads on the abacus. Tell her that as she says each number in the sequence, she should also notice how that number "looks" (or is represented) on the abacus. (The idea is to get her to know not only the digits in the number but also how the number looks when it is represented in other contexts—in relation to 100, in relation to another number in the sequence, etc.) Pick another flash card and repeat the procedure with a different fact.

# Colorful Counting

DEVELOPING/PROFICIENT

INDIVIDUAL OR
SMALL GROUP

Give each child a 100 chart, crayons or markers, and an abacus. Tell the children to color a skip counting sequence of your choice. If the task is to count by 8s to 80, they color in the boxes containing 8, 16, 24, 32, and so forth. Once the coloring is complete, have each child show the same skip counting pattern on the abacus, displaying each number as he says it aloud.

# Skill: Solves basic math problems with manipulatives, then transfers the problems to paper.

A child's ability to work out a problem concretely with manipulatives and then transfer that problem using the abstract (numbers and symbols) is a sign of his deepening understanding of mathematics. The following activities provide practice with each operation and support a seamless transfer of children's numeracy skills to a more sophisticated understanding of number relationships.

## Add 'em Up or Take 'em Away          DEVELOPING
INDIVIDUAL

Cover the sides of two dice with masking tape and write the numbers 10, 20, 30, 40, 50, 60 on one die and 5, 10, 15, 20, 25, 30 on the other. Give the child the dice, an abacus, and paper and pencil. Tell her to roll both dice and use the abacus to find the sum of the two numbers rolled. Once she's shown the number on the abacus, ask her to write the same problem on her paper. Repeat as time allows. Use the same process with subtraction, having her find the difference between the two numbers she rolled.

## Let the Chips Fall          DEVELOPING
INDIVIDUAL

Give the child a 100 chart, two bingo chips, and a dry-erase board and marker. Tell the child to place each chip on a different number, add or subtract the numbers, and then transfer the same problem to the dry-erase board. If you want the number selection to be more varied, you can decide where the chips should fall.

# On the Abacus

**INDIVIDUAL OR SMALL GROUP**

DEVELOPING

Give the child a piece of paper, a pencil, an abacus, and a small pile of flash cards containing addition, subtraction, or multiplication problems. Tell the child to pick one card and solve the problem using his abacus. Then have him transfer the problem to his paper. Repeat as time allows.

# Cubes

**INDIVIDUAL OR SMALL GROUP**

DEVELOPING

Using Unifix cubes, model how to solve a multiplication problem in the form of an array. For example, 4 x 3 would be 4 rows of 3, or 3 + 3 + 3 + 3, so you would link the cubes into 4 groups, with 3 cubes in each. Give the child a pile of the cubes and pose a simple multiplication problem for her to solve. As she becomes more skilled, include larger numbers in the problems and have her transfer each problem onto paper after solving it with the cubes.

# Squared

**INDIVIDUAL OR SMALL GROUP**

DEVELOPING

Give the child a piece of graph paper, blank paper, and a pencil. Model how to use the graph paper to make an array and solve a multiplication problem. Provide him with simple multiplication problems, and after he solves each one, have him write it as a number equation on the blank paper. As he becomes more skilled, use larger numbers in the problems.

# Pay Day

**INDIVIDUAL OR SMALL GROUP**

DEVELOPING

Seat the child at a table with up to 100 play-money one dollar bills and approximately 10 paper plates. Explain and model how to solve a division problem with these materials. For example, if the problem is 18 divided by 3, take 18 dollar bills and set out 3 paper plates. Starting with the first plate, "deal" one of the dollars to each plate, as if dealing cards, until all dollars have been used. Explain that the number of bills on any one plate, in this case 6, is the answer to 18 divided by 3. Repeat with other problems, using larger numbers as the child becomes more skilled, and each time have her show the same problem on paper after she has solved it using manipulatives.

# Work Sheets

**INDIVIDUAL, SMALL GROUP, OR WHOLE GROUP**

DEVELOPING/PROFICIENT

Give each child an abacus, counting frame, or Unifix cubes plus a math work sheet appropriate for their level of readiness. Tell them to solve each problem using the abacus or other tool provided, and then solve the same problem on their paper as well.

# Section 2: Gross Motor Skills

# Gross Motor Skills Profile

Student: _____  Date of Birth: _____

Teacher: _____ Grade: _____  School: _____

Skill

- Walks with balance and spatial awareness.
- Runs well on flat ground.
- Runs well on uneven surfaces.
- Stands with confidence on balance board.
- Jumps on mini-tramp.
- Demonstrates underhand throwing skills.
- Demonstrates catching skills with large ball.
- Demonstrates catching skills with small ball or beanbag.
- Walks on balance beam or line.
- Hops two-legged.
- Hops on alternating feet.
- Balances on one foot with eyes open.
- Balances on one foot with eyes closed (6 or more seconds).
- Demonstrates standing cross-crawl (marching) pattern.
- Dribbles ball with one hand.
- Dribbles ball with alternating hands.
- Skips smoothly for at least 10 yards.
- Demonstrates smooth jumping jacks.

| Beginning | Developing | Proficient |
|---|---|---|
| | | |
| | | |
| | | |
| | | |
| | | |
| | | |
| | | |
| | | |
| | | |
| | | |
| | | |
| | | |
| | | |
| | | |
| | | |
| | | |
| | | |
| | | |

REPRODUCIBLE

# Gross Motor Skills Rubric

| Skill | Beginning | Developing | Proficient |
|---|---|---|---|
| Walks with balance and spatial awareness. | Requires great effort to walk with balance and spatial awareness. | Walks with balance and spatial awareness with some conscious effort. | Easily walks independently with steady balance and spatial awareness. |
| Runs well on flat ground. | Runs with great effort on flat ground. | Runs steadily with some effort on flat ground. | Runs steadily and easily on flat ground for at least 100 feet. |
| Runs well on uneven surfaces. | Runs with great effort on uneven surfaces. | Runs steadily with some effort on uneven surfaces. | Runs steadily and easily on uneven surfaces for at least 100 feet. |
| Stands with confidence on balance board. | Stands with great effort (unbalanced) on balance board. | Stands with some effort on balance board. | Stands calmly and steadily on balance board. |
| Jumps on mini-tramp. | Requires great effort to jump on mini-tramp. | Requires some effort to jump on mini-tramp. | Easily jumps on mini-tramp. |
| Demonstrates underhand throwing skills. | Struggles with simple throwing of ball underhand. | Throws ball underhand in straight line some of the time. | Consistently throws ball underhand to target or person. |
| Demonstrates catching skills with large ball. | Struggles with catching large ball. | Catches large ball some of the time when thrown in straight line. | Catches large ball even when thrown to the side or up in the air. |
| Demonstrates catching skills with small ball or beanbag. | Struggles with catching small ball or beanbag. | Catches small ball or beanbag some of the time when thrown in straight line. | Catches small ball or beanbag even when thrown to the side or up in the air. |
| Walks on balance beam or line. | Balances unsteadily walking on balance beam or line. Frequently falls to the side. | Can walk forward the length of 10-foot balance beam or line, but is unsteady. | Has steady balance walking forward or backward on 10-foot balance beam or line. |
| Hops two-legged. | Struggles with hopping. Cannot hop 3–4 times in one direction. | Hops 3–6 times in one direction. | Sustains hopping for 15 seconds. |

REPRODUCIBLE

| | | | |
|---|---|---|---|
| Hops on alternating feet. | Struggles to stand on one foot and hop to the other foot. | Stands on one foot and hops to the other foot 3–6 times. | Sustains alternate-foot hopping for 15 seconds. |
| Balances on one foot with eyes open. | Unsteady when standing on one foot. Frequently puts other foot on floor to find balance. | Can stand on one foot for 6–10 seconds, with wobbling and adjusting position. | Stands steadily on one foot for 6–10 seconds. |
| Balances on one foot with eyes closed (6 or more seconds). | Unsteady when standing on one foot with eyes closed. Frequently puts other foot on floor to find balance. | Stands steadily on one foot with eyes closed for 2–3 seconds. | Stands steadily on one foot with eyes closed for 6 seconds. |
| Demonstrates standing cross-crawl (marching) pattern. | Struggles to touch hand to opposite knee when marching. | Touches hand to opposite knee when marching, but not with ease and rhythm. | Touches hand to opposite knee with ease and rhythm when marching. |
| Dribbles ball with one hand. | Struggles to control ball when dribbling with one hand. | Dribbles ball while looking at it and giving task full attention. | Dribbles ball easily without looking at it for 15 seconds. |
| Dribbles ball with alternating hands. | Struggles to control ball when dribbling with alternating hands. | Uses alternating hands to dribble ball while looking at it and giving task full attention. | Uses alternating hands to dribble ball while looking at it for 15 seconds. |
| Skips smoothly for at least 10 yards. | Unable to skip. May gallop instead. | Skips deliberately or awkwardly. | Skips with smooth rhythm and gait for 10 yards or more. |
| Demonstrates smooth jumping jacks. | Struggles to coordinate hands and feet in unison. | Does jumping jacks deliberately and with great concentration. | Easily does 10 or more smooth jumping jacks. |

# Procedures for Assessment of Gross Motor Skills

| Skill | Procedures for Assessment | Standards for Proficiency |
|---|---|---|
| Walks with balance and spatial awareness. | Have child walk a distance greater than 100 feet over an outdoor play surface without prompts or assistance. | Easily walks independently with steady balance and spatial awareness. |
| Runs well on flat ground. | Have child run a distance of at least 100 feet over a flat play surface without prompts or assistance. | Runs steadily and easily on flat ground for at least 100 feet. |
| Runs well on uneven surfaces. | Have child run a distance of at least 100 feet over an outdoor play surface without prompts or assistance. | Runs steadily and easily on uneven surfaces for at least 100 feet. |
| Stands with confidence on balance board. | Have child step independently onto balance board and stand or rock comfortably for one minute or longer. | Stands calmly and steadily on balance board. |
| Jumps on mini-tramp. | Have child step independently onto mini-tramp and jump safely and continuously at least 20 times. | Easily jumps on mini-tramp. |
| Demonstrates underhand throwing skills. | Using small, soft ball or beanbag, have child throw underhand to you at a distance of 10 feet. | Consistently throws ball underhand to target or person. |
| Demonstrates catching skills with large ball. | Using large playground ball or basketball, have child catch balls thrown to the middle, each side, and up in the air. | Catches large ball even when thrown to the side or up in the air. |
| Demonstrates catching skills with small ball or beanbag. | Using small, soft ball or beanbag, have child catch balls thrown to the middle, to each side, and into the air slightly above his head, at a distance of 10 feet. | Catches small ball or beanbag even when thrown to the side or up in the air. |

REPRODUCIBLE

| | | |
|---|---|---|
| Walks on balance beam or line. | Have child step independently onto balance beam or line, and walk its length forward and backward without falling off. | Has steady balance walking forward or backward on 10-foot balance beam or line. |
| Hops two-legged. | Have child hop, two-legged, for a distance of 10 feet or more. | Sustains hopping for 15 seconds. |
| Hops on alternating feet. | Have child hop from one foot to the other, and sustain movement for at least 15 seconds. | Sustains alternate-foot hopping for 15 seconds. |
| Balances on one foot with eyes open. | Have child stand on flat surface, choose either foot to raise, and balance on one foot for at least 6 seconds. | Stands steadily on one foot for 6–10 seconds. |
| Balances on one foot with eyes closed (6 or more seconds). | Have child stand on flat surface, choose either foot to raise, and balance on one foot with eyes closed for at least 6 seconds. | Stands steadily on one foot with eyes closed for 6 seconds. |
| Demonstrates standing cross-crawl (marching) pattern. | Standing on flat surface, have child march in cross-crawl pattern, touching hand to opposite knee, in rhythm, for at least 30 seconds. | Touches hand to opposite knee with ease and rhythm when marching. |
| Dribbles ball with one hand. | Using basketball or playground ball, have child dribble ball without stopping for at least 15 seconds. | Dribbles ball easily without looking at it for 15 seconds. |
| Dribbles ball with alternating hands. | Using basketball or playground ball, have child dribble ball using alternating hands without stopping for at least 15 seconds. | Uses alternating hands to dribble ball while looking at it for 15 seconds. |
| Skips smoothly for at least 10 yards. | Standing on flat surface, have child skip smoothly and without stopping to designated goal. Make sure goal is at least 10 yards away and surface is even and uncluttered. | Skips with smooth rhythm and gait for 10 yards or more. |
| Demonstrates smooth jumping jacks. | Have child do 10 or more jumping jacks. | Easily does 10 or more smooth jumping jacks. |

# Activities for Building GROSS MOTOR SKILLS

Children learn best when activities offer a bit of challenge in combination with lots of success. If you keep the sessions simple, fun, and successful, they will want more motor skill practice. Praise their efforts; encourage that next hop, leap, or jump. And look for ways to incorporate academic concepts into your practice sessions to add to the excitement and the joy of learning. Many of the following activities can be done throughout the day, whenever you have a few extra minutes—as part of a transition to another space or when your children just need a minute or two to move their bodies.

# Skill: Walks with balance and spatial awareness.

As a child develops gross motor skills, she learns to move her body at various speeds with the correct amount of force, while maintaining awareness of her own stability and the surrounding environment. Walking with balance in different spaces is one of the foundation skills for many other gross motor tasks, so don't skip over this skill. To ensure success, teach good walking posture: head up, eyes looking in the direction where you're walking, feet straight ahead, and arms swinging in opposition to the legs.

## The Two-Step

BEGINNING

**INDIVIDUAL OR SMALL GROUP**

Give each child two carpet squares, two pieces of construction paper, or two sheets of newspaper. Mark a starting point and an ending point in your room. Tell them that they are to move from one point to the other by walking only on their squares. Model how to lay down one square, take a step, lay down the second square, turn around to pick up the first one, and then take another step. Have children travel across the room in this fashion to the specified destination.

## Human Checkers

BEGINNING

**INDIVIDUAL**

Create a checkerboard pattern in your work or rug area with tape, linoleum tiles, construction paper, or carpet squares, making each space about one foot square. Have the child stand in the center square, and then tell him where and how to move with directions such as: move backward one space, move to the right two spaces, or move forward three spaces. As the child improves at regaining or keeping his balance after each action, begin giving him two directions in a row. To add another dimension to this activity, put a letter, number, color, or shape on each square, and ask the child to read or identify what's on it as he moves according to your directions. Be sure the child is facing the squares the right way so he's not trying to read sideways or upside down.

# Pass It On

**SMALL GROUP OR WHOLE GROUP**

BEGINNING

Arrange the children in a circle. Tell them that when you say the name of a part of the body, such as elbow, you will use your elbow to touch the elbow of the child standing to your right. Then she will do the same with her elbow to the classmate on her right, and so on around the circle until the "pass-along" comes back to you. Then name another part of the body and do the same with it. In the beginning, name parts of the body that allow the children to keep both feet on the floor and build their sense of space. As they increase in skill (they are no longer elbowing their neighbor in the belly by accident, for example), include "pass-alongs" that require them to balance on one leg briefly, such as "passing the knee."

# At a Standstill

**INDIVIDUAL, SMALL GROUP, OR WHOLE GROUP**

BEGINNING

Model a variety of "statue" positions for the children and allow them time to mimic each one. Then tell them to walk around your space until you say the word "Freeze!" Then they stop and make one of the statue positions you showed them and hold it for a count of three, five, or ten seconds (start with three to build confidence and success). When you say "Unfreeze!" they start moving again until you say "Freeze!" and they must make another statue position. Statue positions might include holding one leg off the ground and the arms straight out to the side; spreading the legs apart and holding the arms straight up in the air; doing an exaggerated "creeping up on someone" position; or placing an elbow to a knee with the head resting on the palm of the hand.

# Heads Up

**BEGINNING/DEVELOPING**

INDIVIDUAL, SMALL GROUP,
OR WHOLE GROUP

Give each child a pair of socks folded together or a beanbag to place on her head. In the beginning, have the children stand still and see how long they can keep the object in place. As they become proficient with that skill, add simple movements, such as taking two steps to the side or shuffling backward or forward. Next, tell them to move from one place in the room to another. Continue challenging them with other body actions like clapping, tapping one shoulder with the opposite hand, lifting one knee, making arm circles, and so on. Join in yourself and allow the children to tell you what to do as you attempt to do the same "balancing acts."

# Speedsters

**BEGINNING/DEVELOPING**

INDIVIDUAL OR SMALL GROUP

Take children outside or into the gymnasium and teach them several different speeds for walking. Assign a number for each speed. At first, keep it simple and use three speeds: low (1), medium (5), and high (10). As the children's ability to change speed becomes more fluid, start adding in-between speeds like medium-low (3) or medium-high (7). Play music if possible and have them walk at various speeds until the music stops.

# Turn and Freeze

**DEVELOPING**

SMALL GROUP OR WHOLE GROUP

Play music and have the children walk around the room, moving among desks, chairs, tables, and each other without touching anything. When the music stops, have them turn quickly but carefully to the opposite direction and freeze until the music begins. Start the music again and repeat the process. Play different types of music while doing the activity and have the children move according to the rhythm or tempo. In addition to changing their speed, the variety of music will keep things interesting. Let them suggest songs they'd like to have you play.

# Locomotion

DEVELOPING

INDIVIDUAL, SMALL GROUP,
OR WHOLE GROUP

Set up chairs, marker cones, or plastic stepping spots in a random pattern on your rug area, in the hallway or gymnasium, or in an outside space. Tell the children to move around these objects in any order or pattern they wish, but without touching them, and to use the form of locomotion you've designated: shuffling feet, walking sideways, walking on tiptoes or heels, etc. Change the locomotion periodically by giving them a freeze signal, a new instruction, and a restart signal. If necessary, model what each kind of travel looks like before having the children do it. This will help with their motor planning. Let the children suggest other ways to travel too, and incorporate those into the movements.

# Crossover Walking

DEVELOPING/PROFICIENT

INDIVIDUAL OR
SMALL GROUP

Draw a line or put a long piece of tape on the ground. Tell the children to walk crossover style along it, with the right foot on the left side of the line and the left foot on the right side of the line. At first, have them do this walking forward. Once they feel comfortable with that, have them try the more difficult task of walking backward in the crossover style. If your children are really up for a challenge, ask them to do this with a beanbag balanced on their heads.

# Rollin', Rollin', Rollin'

DEVELOPING/PROFICIENT

INDIVIDUAL OR SMALL GROUP

Gather the children in a spacious area, like a hallway, gymnasium, or playground. Give each one a hula hoop. Tell them to roll their hoops beside them as they walk along, using the hand they write with. Once they are comfortable and their movements are fluid, challenge them to increase their speed. When a child has mastered this, have her try rolling the hoop with her other hand as she moves along.

## Skill: Runs well on flat ground.

When children first begin to learn how to run, they tend to look at their feet. Allow this at first, but then encourage them to keep their heads up and their eyes looking forward as they become more skilled. Also, be sure that as they run, their toes are facing straight ahead, their knees and elbows are making nearly right angles, their legs and arms are working in opposition, and they are looking ahead instead of turning their heads to either side. In addition, have them practice on even surfaces such as hallways, gymnasiums, or level concrete outside. Playground areas or grassy fields generally do not provide the right conditions for beginners.

## Make a Face, Run in Place

BEGINNING

INDIVIDUAL, SMALL GROUP, OR WHOLE GROUP

Running in place allows a child to get used to the motions of his arms and legs before he has to worry about moving forward. Set up a practice area that's safe and has sufficient space. Mark off a square approximately two feet by two feet with tape on your rug or place a piece of carpet securely on the floor. Tell the children that when you say "Start!" they are to make a silly face and then start running in place, within the confines of the designated space, until you say "Stop!" Repeat the process as long as their stamina allows, always watching for proper running posture.

## Keep the Beat

BEGINNING

INDIVIDUAL, SMALL GROUP, OR WHOLE GROUP

Gather the children in a place with a level, even surface where they have room to walk, such as a hallway, gymnasium, or on concrete outside. Using rhythm sticks (borrowed from your music teacher) or wooden blocks, beat a rhythm to set the walking speed for the children. Start slowly and tell them to walk in time to your beat. As you increase the beat, they increase their walking speed. Get them walking as fast as they can without actually running.

# Walk 'n Run

INDIVIDUAL, SMALL GROUP,
OR WHOLE GROUP

BEGINNING/DEVELOPING

Bring the children to an area where they will have room to both walk and run safely for short distances. Explain to them that every time you give a signal (blow a whistle or ring a bell), they will change the action that they are engaged in. Model this for them: give the signal and start to walk, give the signal again and start to run, give the signal a third time and return to walking. Repeat until the children understand how the game works. Then line them up at one end of your work area, give the signal, and have them start walking. After a few seconds, signal again and make sure they begin to run. You can also have them do this between obstacles. Set up chairs, cones, or plastic stepping spots, and tell them to move around them using the action you signal. As a variation, tell the children to change actions each time you say, for example, a word that rhymes with "flat" or ends with "er," or a number that is greater than 6.

# Hold That Pose

INDIVIDUAL, SMALL GROUP,
OR WHOLE GROUP

BEGINNING/DEVELOPING

In order for children to run smoothly, they need to have their arms moving in opposition to their legs and their elbows and knees making nearly right angles. To be sure the children are doing this correctly, have them start running and periodically tell them to freeze and hold their position. Check to see if they have the right form and make adjustments as necessary. After a few seconds, give the signal for them to start running again, and after a few seconds more, tell them to freeze. Repeat until you have been able to check each one.

# Knee Highs

**INDIVIDUAL, SMALL GROUP, OR WHOLE GROUP**

DEVELOPING

Have children jog in place with their hands held out in front of them at waist level. Then tell them to let their left knee hit their left hand or their right knee hit their right hand each time they raise a leg. Encourage them to keep their heads up and eyes looking forward while they do this to prepare them for the addition of forward movement at a later point.

# Simon Says

**INDIVIDUAL OR SMALL GROUP**

DEVELOPING

Do this on a level surface where the children can run safely and maneuver around a few obstacles. Based on your location (inside or outdoors), you might say something like "Simon says run to the door; Simon says run to me; Run to your desk; Simon says run around the orange cone." Continue to give commands that allow the children to run in spurts to build their confidence, skill, and stamina.

# Copycat

**INDIVIDUAL OR SMALL GROUP**

DEVELOPING/PROFICIENT

Choose an open area with plenty of room for running safely. Tell the children that they are to watch what you do and then do the same thing themselves. For example, you might run at different speeds, then on your tiptoes, and then with knees high; or jog slowly, then jog in place, and then with your arms raised. Keep an eye on each child to make sure he is correctly mimicking each of your movements.

# Obstacle Course Relay

SMALL GROUP

DEVELOPING/PROFICIENT

In an open space, create an obstacle course with cones, plastic stepping spots, chairs, or other objects that children can run around safely. Leave enough room between each obstacle so they can weave their way between them. Divide the children and have them line up at both ends of the course, but allow only one child to travel at a time. Tell her to weave her way through the obstacles as quickly as possible, trying not to touch any. Once she reaches her classmates at the end of the course, the children high five each other and then another one runs the course. Celebrate each child's success.

GROSS MOTOR SKILLS

## Skill: Runs well on uneven surfaces.

Many of the activities found in an earlier skill ("Runs well on flat ground," pages 96–99) will also work well for building this skill. Be sure to keep safety and success in the forefront of your plans for every child, as running on uneven surfaces will require more balance and coordination. Uneven surfaces include outdoor playgrounds, grassy fields, and sandy areas. As always, make sure the children show good running posture, with elbows and knees bent at nearly right angles, arms and legs working in opposition, and eyes looking straight ahead. Playing games during recess that involve running, like tag and soccer, are great ways to reinforce this skill.

# Near and Far

BEGINNING

**SMALL GROUP OR WHOLE GROUP**

Bring the children to an open space with uneven ground. Choose a spot where you will stand during the activity. Explain to the children that you will give them three different verbal cues telling them where or how to run. If you say "near," they are to run toward you. If you say "far," they are to run away from you, and if you say "on the spot," they are to run in place. Standing about 20 feet away from the children, give them a signal and then change it every 10 seconds or so, depending on their stamina.

# Touch and Run

BEGINNING

**INDIVIDUAL OR SMALL GROUP**

Scatter different kinds of objects around your play space, such as a plastic cone, laundry basket, cardboard box, or anything similar that you have on hand. Tell the child that when you call out the name of one of the objects, she is to run to it, touch it, and then wait for your next cue, which will be the name of a different object. As the child becomes more skilled, call out a sequence of objects for her to run to or name the object and tell her what speed to run to it—slow, medium, or fast.

# Infinity Run

**INDIVIDUAL**

DEVELOPING

Place two markers about 10 feet apart on the ground. Model how to run a continuous figure-eight pattern around the markers. Allow the child to power walk or jog at first, if necessary, and encourage him to increase his speed each time he completes the figure eight.

# Tricky Trail

**INDIVIDUAL**

DEVELOPING

Lay out 10 to 20 markers in a pattern on the playground. With chalk or tape, write a different number (1, 2, 3…) on each. Make sure the markers are about 10 feet apart from each other, and mix up the numerical order so the child must search for the one that comes next in sequence. Model how to run around the markers in numerical order, touching each one before moving on to the next. Then have the child do the same. Repeat as her stamina allows.

# This Way and That Way

**INDIVIDUAL**

DEVELOPING/PROFICIENT

Place 8 to 10 plastic cones (or another kind of marker) on the playground or some other spacious, uneven surface. Space each one four to five feet apart. Model how to run a zigzag pattern around the markers from the first one to the last. Have the child jog at first and gradually increase his speed until he's running. Time him, if desired, and challenge him to beat his own record. When he's ready, tell him to run through the markers backward but at a slower pace. Keep things interesting and challenging by decreasing the space between the markers and changing the layout of the course.

# Skill: Stands with confidence on balance board.

Balance board activities require children to ratchet their stability skills "up a notch" and should be started after they have established the ability to balance on steady ground. (A balance board is a rectangular board, approximately 24 x 18 inches, with wooden rockers attached underneath.) When a child is standing on a balance board, she is using both hemispheres of her brain. The result is that information taken in is learned faster and retained longer, with better comprehension. When both sides of the brain are working together, the ability to process, file, and store information is more efficient. So when possible, include exercises such as counting, reading, and spelling in your balance board activities. If you have more than one balance board, you can do some of the following activities safely with small groups.

## Getting Started

BEGINNING

INDIVIDUAL

Let the child explore the balance board by placing one foot on the board and one foot on the floor. Allow him to rock the board from side to side with each foot in turn. Hold the child's hand and help him onto the board. You may need to put one foot under the board to stabilize it while the child is getting on for the first time or so. Encourage him to try to stand steadily on the board and then, when he feels ready, tell him to try rocking it gently from side to side. Assure him that you'll stay nearby in case he needs your hand for support.

# Moving On

BEGINNING/DEVELOPING

INDIVIDUAL OR
SMALL GROUP

As a child's skill on a balance board increases, have her do some movements with her arms or hands, such as using one arm to make the shape of a figure eight in the air, tapping different parts of her body with her hand, or copying a clapping pattern you show her. Next, give her a verbal task to do while balancing, such as singing a song, reciting the alphabet, or skip counting.

# From One Hand to the Other

BEGINNING/DEVELOPING

INDIVIDUAL OR
SMALL GROUP

Have the child steady himself on the balance board and then hand him a beanbag or koosh ball. Tell him to pass the beanbag or ball from one hand to the other while keeping his balance. At first, he might need to hold his hands close together, but as he becomes more proficient, encourage him to increase the distance between them. To challenge him further, tell him to count each toss he makes.

# Balance and Catch

DEVELOPING

INDIVIDUAL

With the child standing on a balance board, play a traditional game of catch with a large playground ball. Tell her to catch the ball and then gently throw it back to you, using an underhand motion. Don't allow wild throws. As her skill increases, decrease the size of the ball or use a beanbag for more of a challenge. Practice throwing to the center of her body, to the sides, and then slightly higher than her head so she has to reach up to catch. Eventually, try using two beanbags or koosh balls, so that each of you can throw and catch in synchrony. Be sure, however, to maintain a high level of success and joy.

# Balance, Catch, and Count

DEVELOPING

INDIVIDUAL

Bring 10 beanbags to the practice area and ask the child to stand on the balance board. Say a number, such as 5, and tell him that you are going to toss him that many beanbags. He is to catch and hold onto them and say "Stop" when he's caught the number you have specified. Then have him throw the beanbags back to you, one at a time, while counting and balancing on the board.

# Add-a-Bounce

DEVELOPING

INDIVIDUAL

Play bounce-and-catch while the child is standing on the balance board. Using a large playground ball, bounce it to her. After she catches the ball, tell her to bounce it back to you, and repeat. As her skill increases, decrease the size of the ball for more of a challenge.

# Target Practice

DEVELOPING/PROFICIENT

INDIVIDUAL OR
SMALL GROUP

Set up a target on the floor using a carpet square or hula hoop and on a wall using a white board or other object. Have the child stand on the balance board and give him a number of beanbags or koosh balls. When he's found his balance, tell him to throw at the various targets. As his skill increases, have him toss the beanbags or balls *into* a target like a bucket or a box. Eventually, challenge him further by specifying which targets to throw at and in what order—for example, "Throw at the green square, then the red circle, then the yellow triangle."

# Up, Up, and Away

INDIVIDUAL

DEVELOPING/PROFICIENT

Have the child steady herself on the board. Give her an inflated balloon and ask her to tap it to you gently with an open hand. Catch the balloon, tap it back to her, and repeat. As she becomes more comfortable, tap the balloon back and forth between you and the child without stopping. Then, when she's ready, have her tap the balloon in the air by herself for as many taps as possible while remaining balanced on the board.

# Getting Creative

INDIVIDUAL

DEVELOPING/PROFICIENT

Place the balance board in front of an easel or magnetic board. Tell the child to stand on the board, find his balance, and then do something creative, such as drawing shapes or pictures while balancing. He can also write letters, numbers, or words. To increase the challenge, play a game like Hangman or Tic-Tac-Toe with him while he maintains his balance on the board.

# Table Games

INDIVIDUAL OR
SMALL GROUP

DEVELOPING/PROFICIENT

With the balance board next to a table, ask the child to build with Legos, stack blocks, or connect Tinker Toys or Unifix cubes while maintaining her balance. Next, play a game of Pickup Sticks or have her deal cards while she balances.

# Skill: Jumps on mini-tramp.

Using a trampoline improves motor skills by forcing the brain to function bilaterally—using both the left and the right sides at the same time. In response to the forces of gravity acting on the body in all directions when you are in the air, both sides of the body and the brain become engaged in maintaining balance and coordination. And that makes for a better brain.

## Starting Out                                                          BEGINNING

INDIVIDUAL

Before engaging in trampoline activities, children need to feel safe and comfortable. Model the best way to get on and off the trampoline, using the handle if yours is equipped with one. Then let the child practice getting on and off as many times as necessary to build confidence. Once he's on comfortably, ask him to stand in place. Then tell him to bounce gently to give him a sense of what it will feel like later when he is ready for active mini-tramp exercises.

## Now You've Got It                                                     BEGINNING

INDIVIDUAL

Have the child get onto the trampoline and allow her some time just to stand on it and get a sense of balance. Then tell her to start bouncing very slightly two or three times (her feet should maintain contact with the surface of the trampoline). Sometimes it's necessary to hold the child's body at the waistline and gently bounce her. When she is comfortable with this motion, have her try bouncing on her own, but stay close by to "spot" her. You can hold her hand lightly in the beginning and gradually release it as she feels more confident. Increase the number of consecutive bounces she attempts, counting them aloud if desired.

# Tippy Toes

INDIVIDUAL

BEGINNING

Ask the child to stand on his toes on solid ground, and then model how to do the same thing on the mini-tramp. Next, have the child do this on the trampoline. Once he has the rhythm, ask him to do five toe-raises, then bounce twice (high enough so his feet leave the surface). Next, have him do six toe-raises, and then bounce a little higher two more times, and so on.

# Mini-Tramp March

INDIVIDUAL

BEGINNING

Have the child stand on the mini-tramp and ask her to lift up one foot and then the other. Repeat this five or six times. Once the child feels comfortable, tell her to stand in the middle of the trampoline and march according to the beat and tempo you create verbally ("left, right, left, right"). Start out slowly, holding her hand if necessary, and increase the speed of your verbal cues as the child gains confidence. If desired, play music that lends itself to marching.

# Walking on the Moon

INDIVIDUAL

BEGINNING

Ask the child to get safely onto the trampoline. Hold his hand and ask him to jump high enough so that both of his feet leave the surface of the trampoline. Once he is comfortable with this bouncing motion, release his hand and have him jump as many consecutive times as he is able. Count the jumps out loud with him, encouraging him to try adding more jumps. Stay nearby to "spot" him in case he loses his balance.

# Forward & Backward

INDIVIDUAL

DEVELOPING

Standing on the mini-tramp, model for the child how to make forward circles with your arms while jumping. Then step off and have the child get on, but tell her to stand still as she makes the arm circles. Once she's mastered that motion, encourage her to start jumping, increasing the size of the circles and the height of the jumps as she becomes more comfortable. To keep things interesting, have her include backward arm circles and then a combination of both directions upon your cue.

# Clapping All the Way

INDIVIDUAL

DEVELOPING

Get the child on the mini-tramp and bouncing at a comfortable pace, and then introduce a clapping motion. Tell him that you are going to give him a cue for the way you want him to clap while he continues jumping. For example, you might say, "Clap once," "Clap twice," "Clap loudly," or "Clap softly." When the child becomes confident with the clapping, challenge him further by telling him to clap behind his back, up high, down low, or to either side of his body.

# Jumping Jack Jam

INDIVIDUAL

DEVELOPING

Have the child do some jumping jacks on solid ground to make sure she knows how to do them. Then have her get on the trampoline and tell her to do half of a jumping jack, landing with her feet apart, and then stop. Next, have her do the other part of a jumping jack, landing with her feet together, and then stop. As she becomes more confident, tell her to increase her jumping speed until she eventually reaches the point of doing complete and consecutive jumping jacks. To keep things fun, play some music with a steady beat that she can jump to.

# Left Leg, Right Leg

INDIVIDUAL

DEVELOPING/PROFICIENT

Have the child stand on the trampoline. Tell her to jump from one foot to the other and then back to the first foot. Repeat the activity until the child is comfortable. Then introduce simple patterns you want her to do as you call out the foot she should use, such as *right, right, left* or *left, left, right*. Increase the difficulty of the patterns as the child becomes more skilled.

# Throw and Catch

INDIVIDUAL

DEVELOPING/PROFICIENT

Have the child get on the mini-tramp and give her a beanbag. Tell her to start jumping and then throw the beanbag to you. While she continues jumping, throw the beanbag back to her. Continue throwing and catching back and forth until she is consistently successful with throwing, catching, and jumping.

# Jumping in a Circle

INDIVIDUAL

DEVELOPING/PROFICIENT

Model how to jump on the mini-tramp while turning your body in a clockwise direction; then do it in a counterclockwise direction. Next, have the child get on the mini-tramp and jump a few times to get his "trampoline legs." Tell him to follow your verbal cues on how far to turn while he's jumping. For example, you might have him turn about a quarter of the way around each time he jumps. After he's completed one or two rotations, ask him to do the same thing in a counterclockwise direction. As his skill increases, give him more challenging directions, such as *a quarter turn right, then left, then left again, then right*. Spot the child carefully since the turning motion could make him dizzy.

# Skill: Demonstrates underhand throwing skills.

In order for children to be successful with underhand throwing, they need to have the correct throwing motion, good arm and shoulder strength, and a proper grip on the object to be thrown. The ball, or whatever the object, should be held mostly with the fingers and not in the palm. Children should be positioned in such a way that they are able to extend their throwing arm back as far as possible, with their eyes on the target, and their feet facing the target. To ensure success, concentrate on technique first, then distance.

## Pretend for Practice                                    BEGINNING

**INDIVIDUAL OR SMALL GROUP**

Model the proper position and movements for underhand throwing and then have the children do the same. Tell them to place their feet in a diagonal stance (one foot in front and one in back) and to rock back and forth to get a sense of the weight shift they'll make when they throw. After practicing this, have them swing their throwing arm back and forth with an empty hand. Next, place a beanbag or koosh ball in each child's hand and ask him to make the throwing motion with the object but not to let it go. Once the children are comfortable with the procedure, allow them time to practice throwing beanbags, koosh balls, or other soft items.

## Partner Pass                                    BEGINNING/DEVELOPING

**INDIVIDUAL OR SMALL GROUP (in pairs)**

Give the child a koosh ball or a beanbag. Have her stand toe to toe with you and then both of you take two steps back. Instruct the child to throw the ball underhand to you with two hands at first. After each of you has thrown the ball once or twice, take another step backward away from each other and continue to throw as before. Once the child is comfortable throwing with two hands, have her practice using only one hand to throw but both hands to catch. If children are doing this in pairs, model the process for them first.

# Hand to Hand

**INDIVIDUAL, SMALL GROUP, OR WHOLE GROUP**

BEGINNING/DEVELOPING

Provide each child with a beanbag, koosh ball, or similar object. Model for them how to toss it underhand from one hand to the other. Start with your hands close together and then gradually move them farther apart. Now have them try this on their own. As their skills increase, ask them to throw the object slightly higher each time they toss it up. For a greater challenge, tell them to count to a certain number or recite the alphabet while throwing the object.

# Wad It Up

**INDIVIDUAL OR SMALL GROUP**

DEVELOPING

Place a large laundry basket at one end of your work area and put a length of tape on the floor as a throwing line. Give the child a sheet of newspaper and have him wad it up to form a ball. Tell him to stand behind the tape line and try to throw the wad of paper into the basket. After he throws, have him retrieve it and repeat the process. Start out with a large laundry basket, but as the child becomes more skilled, use a smaller basket or ask him to stand farther away from it.

# Bowling for Bottles

**INDIVIDUAL OR SMALL GROUP**

DEVELOPING

At one end of your work space, set up 10 empty, two-liter soda bottles in a configuration similar to what you'd see at a bowling alley. Mark off a throwing line on the floor with tape, placing it fairly close to the bottles to start (but progressively moving it farther away as the child's skill improves). Give the child a small playground ball and tell her to roll it toward the soda bottles to see how many she can knock down. Have her count the number of "pins" she bowled over as she sets them back up for the next child. As a variation, write sight words on the pins and ask each child to read them aloud as she sets them up.

# Hole in One

**INDIVIDUAL OR SMALL GROUP**

DEVELOPING

Make a 6-inch-diameter circle with string and place it on the floor in your work space. Take a ball of clay, insert a small paper flag, and set this in the center of the string circle. This is the hole. Give each child a small beanbag and put a carpet square on the floor where the child should stand. This is the tee. In turn, have the children throw their beanbags and try to get them in the hole (inside the string circle), keeping track of how many throws it takes to do this. If children are struggling, make the hole bigger. If you have room, set up more than one hole and let the children play a round of golf.

# Scarf Juggling

**INDIVIDUAL, SMALL GROUP, OR WHOLE GROUP**

PROFICIENT

Provide each child with a lightweight scarf (not a winter scarf). Show them how to toss it underhand into the air and catch it with the same hand, the other hand, or both hands. Allow them to practice for several minutes until they are successful more often than not. Then give each one a second scarf and model how to toss first one in the air and then the second before catching either. The scarves will not go very far or high, which makes it a little easier for the children to keep control of them.

# **Skill:** Demonstrates catching skills with large ball.

In order for children to be successful at catching, they need to learn certain body postures and positions. To begin with, they should face the thrower with their feet spread about shoulder width apart so they have good balance. Their knees and arms should be slightly bent and their fingers relaxed. They also need to keep their eyes on the object being thrown. In the beginning, children tend to catch with their arms and bodies, but as their skills improve, encourage them to catch with their hands and fingers only.

## Roll with It                                                   BEGINNING

INDIVIDUAL OR SMALL GROUP (in pairs)

Ask the child to sit on the floor opposite you and a few feet away, with his legs stretched out in front of him in a V. This will allow the ball to come closer. Roll a large ball toward the child and ask him to scoop it up with both hands and arms, and then roll it back to you. Continue until the child is able to contain the ball each time you roll it. Decrease the size of the ball slightly as his skill increases and he is using his arms less and his hands more. If you are doing this activity with pairs of children, model the actions first. For a greater challenge, tell the children to recite the alphabet or count to a certain number while rolling the ball back and forth.

## Old Softy                                                      BEGINNING

INDIVIDUAL OR SMALL GROUP

In order for children to be able to catch successfully, they need to be relaxed and ready. Sometimes the hardness of a ball makes it difficult for a child to catch, and sometimes they have a fear of being hit by a ball. If this is the case, give each child a large stuffed animal. Have them practice throwing it to each other, up in the air and catching it themselves, or catching it as you throw it to them from different distances or positions. As they become more comfortable and successful, begin adding a large, soft ball for them to practice with as well.

# Ball Bonanza

BEGINNING/DEVELOPING

INDIVIDUAL OR
SMALL GROUP

Use a playground ball that is 12 to 16 inches in diameter. Ask the child to stand and face you, leaving only about three feet between you. Tell the child to get ready to catch, and then gently and slowly throw the ball underhand to her. This gives her a chance to follow the ball with her eyes more easily. Now ask her to throw it back to you underhand. Gradually increase the distance and the speed with which you throw the ball, and keep on playing catch as her stamina allows and she continues to experience success.

# Throw It to Yourself

BEGINNING/DEVELOPING

INDIVIDUAL, SMALL GROUP,
OR WHOLE GROUP

Gather the children in an area where they can move around safely and not bump into each other or any furniture. Give each one a large ball and tell them to throw the balls up in the air and catch them with both hands. As they get better at catching, encourage them to throw the balls higher. Next, have them add an action while their ball is in the air, such as clapping their hands once or letting it bounce once before they catch it. Model the activity first to be sure everyone understands what to do.

# Balloons for Beginners

BEGINNING/DEVELOPING

INDIVIDUAL, SMALL GROUP,
OR WHOLE GROUP

Balloons are great for catching practice because their slow rate of travel gives children more time to react. Supply each child with an inflated balloon and plenty of room to move around; a gymnasium or playground area is best. Ask them to toss their balloons into the air as high as they can and then catch them.

# Buddy Ball

DEVELOPING

INDIVIDUAL, SMALL GROUP (in pairs),
OR WHOLE GROUP (in pairs)

Give each pair a large ball like a beach ball or a playground ball. (If you are working with just one child, you will be his partner.) With partners standing about three feet apart, have them toss the ball back and forth to one another. After three successful catch-and-throw completions in a row, tell the children to take one baby step backward and continue throwing and catching. When partners are successful most of the time, have each child take one step back every time he gets ready to throw the ball to his partner. If one partner misses two catches in a row, he can take a step closer to his partner if he wishes.

# Bouncing Around

DEVELOPING

INDIVIDUAL, SMALL GROUP (in pairs),
OR WHOLE GROUP (in pairs)

Give each pair a playground ball or basketball. (If you are working with just one child, you will be his partner.) Ask partners to stand face to face about three feet apart. Have one child bounce the ball to the other child, who will try to catch it and then bounce it back to his partner. After five successful bounces and catches, tell them to take a step back and continue. Partners can try to bounce the ball more than once between catches, or they can try to make it bounce higher. Encourage children to catch with their hands instead of with their arms and bodies as they become more skilled.

# Coming Up Short

**DEVELOPING**

INDIVIDUAL

Bring the child and a playground ball to an open space in a hallway, gymnasium, or outside. Stand about five or six feet away from him and tell him to catch the ball when you throw it to him. Throw it in front of him but far enough away so that he'll have to move his body forward to catch the ball. Continue at a variety of distances until the child is able to make the adjustments necessary to catch the ball consistently. As he becomes more skilled, begin throwing the ball slightly beyond where he is standing so he has to back up in order to catch it.

# Wall Ball

**DEVELOPING/PROFICIENT**

INDIVIDUAL OR SMALL GROUP

Provide the child with a large playground ball and an empty expanse of wall. A hallway wall or outside wall works well. Model how to throw the ball gently at the wall and then catch it. In the beginning, it may be easier for him to let the ball bounce once before trying to catch it. As he becomes more skilled, tell him to stand farther away from the wall and to try catching the ball without letting it bounce.

# Catching in Circles

**DEVELOPING/PROFICIENT**

INDIVIDUAL

With string, chalk, or tape, create a circle that is about five feet in diameter. Tell the child to stand in a particular spot inside the circle, where he will stay until you give him a different instruction. Standing outside of the circle, toss a playground ball to him and have him throw it back to you. Quickly change your position around the circle's circumference and throw the ball back to the child. Throw it at different heights and toward different parts or sides of him. Continue increasing speed, direction, and distance as the child's success rate increases.

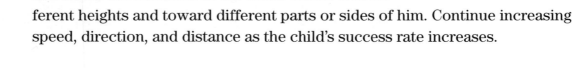

# Skill: Demonstrates catching skills with small ball or beanbag.

When you're having children transfer their catching skills to smaller balls, use koosh balls or beanbags because they have a little "give" to them, unlike tennis balls which are rigid and more difficult to catch. As children become more proficient, however, do incorporate firmer balls. Make sure children continue to exhibit the same posture and position as they used for catching large balls: feet apart, arms and knees slightly bent, hands and fingers relaxed, and eyes on the object being thrown.

## So Big

**INDIVIDUAL**

BEGINNING

Gather a variety of small balls and beanbags that vary slightly in size. With the child facing you and standing about two feet away, hold up one of the balls. Ask her to show you about how far apart her hands should be in order to catch this particular ball. Bring the ball to her hands to see how accurate she was. Repeat with other balls until the child's judgment is more consistent. Using the same balls, throw them to her one at a time to catch.

## The Juggler

**INDIVIDUAL, SMALL GROUP, OR WHOLE GROUP**

BEGINNING

Give each child a beanbag or koosh ball. Model for them how to toss it between both hands, either slightly up in the air or back and forth horizontally. Then have the children try it themselves, challenging them to increase the number of consecutive catches they are able to make. As they become more comfortable with this action, encourage them to increase the distance between their hands or how high they are tossing it into the air, or to count a number sequence while "juggling."

**GROSS MOTOR SKILLS**

# Toss and Touch

BEGINNING

INDIVIDUAL, SMALL GROUP, OR WHOLE GROUP

Bring the children to a space where they will have plenty of room to move around. Give each one a small balloon and allow them time to practice throwing it in the air and catching it. Once they are comfortable with that action, tell them to throw it a bit higher and touch a part of their body, like their shoulder or knee, before catching the balloon.

# Bouncing Baby Ball

BEGINNING/DEVELOPING

INDIVIDUAL, SMALL GROUP (in pairs), OR WHOLE GROUP (in pairs)

Give each child a tennis or racquet ball and have them spread out. Tell them to bounce their balls once and then catch them with both hands. Model this if necessary. When they can do this consistently, challenge them to bounce the balls and catch them with their dominant hand only. If you are working with a group of children, have them pair up and give each pair one ball. Let them work on their own, bouncing their balls back and forth with their partners, first catching the partner's bounce with two hands and then with only one. As the children develop this skill, tell them to throw the ball in the air to themselves or to a partner, catching first with two hands and then with one.

# Got Milk?

DEVELOPING

INDIVIDUAL

Cut the top off an empty gallon milk jug, keeping the handle intact so it resembles a scoop. Give it to the child and have him stand about two feet away, facing you. Tell him to use the jug to try to catch the beanbag (or koosh ball) that you are going to toss to him. Whether he is successful or not, have him retrieve the object and throw it back to you. Continue until he is able to catch it consistently. Then increase the distance between you and the child, the speed at which you throw, or the placement of your throw (slightly above his head, just in front of him, off to one side, etc.).

# Triple Play or Four Square

DEVELOPING

SMALL GROUPS

Ask the children to create a triangle (if there are three of them) or a square (if there are four) with their bodies. Tell them to stand about three giant steps away from each other. Give each group a small playground ball or a tennis ball. Tell one child in each group to throw the ball to the child on her left. That child will catch it and throw it to the child on his left. Children continue to throw the ball in a clockwise direction until you call "Reverse!" at which point they will start tossing it in a counterclockwise direction to the person on their right.

# Partner Wall Ball

DEVELOPING/PROFICIENT

INDIVIDUAL OR SMALL GROUP (in pairs)

Take the child (or pair of children) to a wall in the hallway or outside. Give the child or pair a small playground ball or a tennis ball. Model how to throw the ball underhand at the wall gently and then catch it. Tell the child to throw the ball at the wall and let you (or his partner) catch it. Once the partner has caught the ball, he gently throws it back at the wall. Partners take turns throwing and catching to avoid any unintended bumping or falling. Letting the ball bounce before catching it is an option for children who need that extra reaction time.

# Crazy Catcher

DEVELOPING/PROFICIENT

INDIVIDUAL, SMALL GROUP, OR WHOLE GROUP

Give children beanbags or koosh balls and have them practice catching with both hands. When they are comfortable, ask them to throw their ball in the air and catch it with just one hand. Challenge them to find interesting ways to throw and then catch the beanbags or balls, such as placing it on a foot, tossing it up, and catching it with one hand. Continue with other "crazy catches" like throwing it in the air and catching it behind the back; throwing it, turning all the way around, and then catching it; and throwing it, clapping under a leg once, and catching it. Allow children to create their own safe challenges as well.

# Skill: Walks on balance beam or line.

Consistent balance on a narrow surface requires a lot of practice and develops in stages. With rich movement experiences, children will develop static balance (standing still) and dynamic balance (moving). As children progress, model proper balancing posture: arms out for balance, eyes looking ahead, upper body steady, and knees relaxed. Remember, successful learning experiences will build skills faster than failures, so do not push children further than they are ready to go at any point during these activities.

## Along the Line

**BEGINNING**

INDIVIDUAL

Tape a line on the floor in your work area, making it as wide as necessary to ensure success for the child. (You can also tape two parallel lines for the child to walk *between*.) Holding the child's hand very lightly, guide her as she walks along the line. Continue walking in this manner until she is able to make it all the way to the end without squeezing or grabbing your hand for support. When she's reached that point, have her walk the line without holding onto your hand. Assure her that you will be right there if she needs you for balance at any time. As her success rate increases, gradually move farther away from her. Once the child is comfortable, have her do the same activity on a balance beam, providing her with support as before.

## From Thick to Thin

**BEGINNING**

INDIVIDUAL OR SMALL GROUP

Tape a line about six to twelve feet long on the floor in your work area, using two to three strips of tape to make it extra wide. If you are working with more than one child, create several of these lines to use simultaneously. Ask the children to walk quickly on the line and to try to avoid stepping off it. When they get to the end, have them turn around and walk back to the beginning. As the children become more secure in their ability to stay on the line, decrease its width and have them walk on it with slow, controlled movements.

# Alligator Alley

BEGINNING

INDIVIDUAL OR
SMALL GROUP

Lay a path of plastic stepping spots ("the rocks") in a straight line across your work area ("the river"), leaving a little space between each spot. Tell the child to get across the river by walking only on the path of rocks to avoid the alligators that are lurking just below the surface of the water. If he steps off a rock into the river at any time, have him go back to the beginning and start again. As the child becomes more skilled at crossing the river in one attempt, keep the path straight but either increase the space between the rocks or tell him to walk faster. As a variation, have the child cross the river on tiptoes or heels, or stagger the rocks so the child has to plan his steps. If you have enough stepping spots and more than one child doing this activity at a time, set up multiple paths for them to use simultaneously.

# Stay on Track

BEGINNING

INDIVIDUAL OR
SMALL GROUP

Place two straight, parallel lines of tape on the floor in your work area, or take the children outside and use chalk lines or lengths of rope. At first, make the space between the lines fairly wide, up to 12 inches. Tell the children to "chug" along inside the tracks, avoiding derailment (stepping onto or outside the tracks). If desired, they can make chugging or choo-choo sounds as they go, move their arms to mimic the wheels on a train, or sing a train-related song they know. Any of these will help them develop a rhythm—and stay on track! Once they are able to do this with ease, decrease the space between the tracks and continue to reduce the width until it is only a bit wider than their shoes.

# Look at Me

**INDIVIDUAL**

DEVELOPING

As children become more skilled at walking on a line or balance beam, encourage them to look up as they walk, instead of at their feet. For this activity, stand at one end of the line or beam and tell the child to begin traveling toward you. After she takes a few steps say, "Look at me while you take the next step." If she falls off the line while attempting this, encourage her to get back on at the point where she fell off and try again. When she's successful with one step, encourage her to take two steps, then three, and so on. Finally, challenge her to walk the entire line or beam while looking at you until she's reached you at the other end.

# Variations on a Beam

**INDIVIDUAL**

DEVELOPING/PROFICIENT

Set up a 10- to 20-foot-long line or balance beam and have the child practice walking at different paces, frontward and backward, with normal steps and large steps and heel-to-toe. Walking slowly is more difficult than walking quickly on the line. Practice two to three minutes with just enough challenge but lots of success.

# Mother May I?

**INDIVIDUAL**

DEVELOPING/PROFICIENT

Tape a line or place a balance beam in your work area. Explain how to play "Mother May I?" to the child. Be sure to model what kinds of steps the child may request (this may be based on his level of skill), such as giant, baby, sideways, etc. Have him demonstrate each kind of step before trying it on the balance beam. Once he is secure doing them, have him start at one end of the line or beam, take the steps that are allowed, and try to reach the other end without falling off. As he hones this skill, say no to requests for taking simple steps. For example, if he asks to take one baby step, you might reply, "No, you may not, but you may take one giant step sideways."

# Crossover Balance Line

INDIVIDUAL

DEVELOPING/PROFICIENT

Using a 10- to 20-foot-long line, have the child practice walking it with crossover steps. Each step taken with the left foot ends on the right side of the line, and each step taken with the right foot ends on the left side of the line. Because this requires crossing the midline, it adds an extra element of challenge to the task. As her skills develop, have the child walk at different paces and forward and backward. Practice for two to three minutes with just enough challenge and lots of success.

# Skill: Hops two-legged.

Hopping on two legs is a strenuous activity for many children, so keep sessions short or mix in other locomotion skills that children have already mastered to reduce fatigue and increase feelings of success. As they become better at two-legged hopping, encourage children to keep their feet closer together, as that increases the difficulty of the following tasks.

## Hop in Place Plus

BEGINNING

INDIVIDUAL, SMALL GROUP, OR WHOLE GROUP

Be sure the area you're working in is free of obstacles. Model for the children what hopping on two legs looks like and allow them to try it on their own. Once they are comfortable with the action, begin to give specific directives, such as hop once, hop twice, hop in place to the count of 10, hop in place while reciting the alphabet, etc.

## Hoppin' to the Rhythm

BEGINNING

INDIVIDUAL, SMALL GROUP, OR WHOLE GROUP

This activity is similar to jump rope activities that use rhymes or songs except you will not use a rope. Instead, you and the children will recite a song and hop to the beat. Chants like "A, My Name is Alice" or "Teddy Bear, Teddy Bear" work particularly well. As you recite, you may want to keep the beat by clapping so they get a sense of when they should be hopping. When you first start, keep the beat on the slow side, increasing the tempo as they are able to manage a faster pace.

# Mix It Up

**BEGINNING**

INDIVIDUAL, SMALL GROUP,
OR WHOLE GROUP

Bring the children into a large open area, such as a gymnasium or a playing field. Have them find a starting point they like. Tell them to hop on two legs until you give a signal (a whistle, for example) and your next direction, which might be to walk, tiptoe, run, or any other form of movement they are able to do with ease. Alternate between hopping and other locomotion skills, so they are getting as much hopping practice as possible.

# Climbing the Ladder

**BEGINNING/DEVELOPING**

INDIVIDUAL

Using tape, mark the outline of a ladder on the floor of your work space, making the "rungs" fairly close together. Start the child at one end of the ladder and ask him to hop, two-legged, to the next rung. Have him hop one rung at a time until he does so with ease. Increase the complexity by asking him to hop on a certain number of rungs consecutively or to do something like step on one, hop on two. Again, keep the success rate high. Eventually ask the child to hop on as many consecutive rungs as he can, until he's able to hop the length of the ladder without stopping. To increase the challenge, remove every other rung from the ladder by pulling up alternate pieces of tape.

# Hop Along

**BEGINNING/DEVELOPING**

INDIVIDUAL OR SMALL GROUP

Place colored plastic stepping spots in a random but "hoppable" pattern in your work area. Have the child start on a specific color spot, and then direct her hops from there. For example, if you say "Hop to the blue spot," she locates the nearest blue spot and hops as many times as needed to get to it. Then you might say "Hop to black then red" or "Hop to green then yellow." Start out by having the child hop to spots that are close to her current position. As she becomes more confident, make your directions more challenging. You can do this simultaneously with a small group of children by giving each child her own set of spots appropriately placed.

# Hop and Kick

**INDIVIDUAL OR SMALL GROUP**

DEVELOPING

Bring the child to an open space like a field or gymnasium. Give him a small playground ball, beanbag, or koosh ball. Model this activity before asking the child to complete it. First, kick the ball lightly and then hop to where it landed. Kick it again, hop to it, and so on. Once he's watched you complete a few actions, tell him to pick up where you left off. As he becomes comfortable with this, encourage him to kick the object harder, sending it farther away from him and hopping longer distances to reach it.

# Hopping Hollywood Squares

**INDIVIDUAL**

DEVELOPING

Create a grid of nine or more squares on the floor of your work space or on a paved area outside. The squares should each be about one-foot square. Have the child stand in the middle square and tell him where to hop. For example, you might direct the child to hop forward once, to the left once, then diagonally twice, forward twice, backward once, and so on. Give the directions slowly at first and keep the child hopping forward, sideways, backward, or diagonally.

# Hop and Seek

**INDIVIDUAL**

DEVELOPING

Begin with a small work area. At one end of it, place a pile of different shaped blocks. With the child at the other end, instruct him to hop to the pile, find a rectangular block (for example), and hop back to you with the block. Repeat this according to the child's stamina or success. As he becomes stronger, increase the distance between him and the pile of blocks at the other end.

# Hop, of Course!

INDIVIDUAL OR
SMALL GROUP

DEVELOPING/PROFICIENT

Create a simple obstacle course where children will be able to hop between, around, or through objects. For example, use items such as chairs they can hop around in an S shape, a box they can hop around two times, some plastic stepping spots they can hop onto, a taped line they can hop to the left or right of, and so on. In between each hopping task, allow them to walk or use some other method of locomotion to get to the next part of the course to reduce fatigue.

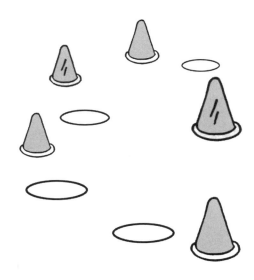

**Skill:** Hops on alternating feet.

Hopping on alternating feet requires good balance and strong legs. If a child is struggling with this, refer to "Hops two-legged" (pages 124–127) and "Balances on one foot with eyes open" (pages 132–135) to build these skills. In addition, point out good hopping posture for children who are unable to do this with ease: the knee of the leg not hopping is bent and used for momentum, the elbows form right angles, the body is leaning slightly forward, and the eyes are looking ahead. Model what good hopping looks like and use verbal cues and reinforcement on a regular basis.

# Stay Put
BEGINNING

INDIVIDUAL OR SMALL GROUP

Before asking a child to move around while hopping on one foot, have him practice hopping on one foot in place. Stand next to the child, supporting one arm, and have him hop on one foot two or three times, and then switch and do the same thing on the other foot. Have him alternate between his two feet to build strength on both sides. When he is comfortable with that, stand far enough away so that he can reach you only with outstretched arm, and ask him to repeat the hops on each foot. A child may also be comfortable holding on to a chalk ledge or a door frame while getting his hopping legs in shape.

# Hop with Me
BEGINNING

INDIVIDUAL

Bring the child to an open area where you have set up a few markers such as cones or plastic stepping spots. Model hopping on one foot from one marker to the next. Then have her take your hand as you both hop on one foot to a marker of her choice. Using the other foot, hop to the next marker in the same manner. Once she is feeling more confident, tell her that you will both hop to the next marker but this time you won't hold hands. As her success rate increases, ask her to choose her next marker and hop to it by herself. If desired, write or attach words, letters, numbers, or shapes on the markers and ask her to identify what's on each one as she hops along.

# Number Jumping

**INDIVIDUAL OR SMALL GROUP**

BEGINNING

Place 10 plastic stepping spots, each with a different number written on it, on the floor in a slightly random pattern and out of numerical order. Make sure the spots are positioned so that the child can hop easily from one to the next. Have the child stand in front of the spot with the number 1 on it. Tell her to hop on one foot from 1 to 2, then 2 to 3, and continue all the way to 10. Then have her hop from 1 to 10 on the other foot. Have older children or those with good number sense use alternate feet as they hop on odd numbers only, even numbers only, or any other criteria you choose. If you have enough spots, you can do this with two or three children simultaneously.

# One Foot, Two Feet

**INDIVIDUAL, SMALL GROUP, OR WHOLE GROUP**

BEGINNING/DEVELOPING

Bring the children to an open space, such as a gymnasium or an outside play area. Explain to them that each time you blow your whistle, you are going to give them directions on how to hop, alternating between hopping on one foot and two feet. Tell them they will know what to do by listening to you. Start with two-feet hopping. After a couple of hops, blow your whistle and call out, for example, "left foot hop" or just "left." Then after another couple of hops you might say, "right foot" or "both feet." Continue the activity as their stamina allows, being sure to alternate between left and right feet when the children are engaged in single-foot hops.

GROSS MOTOR SKILLS

# Hop-a-Line

BEGINNING/DEVELOPING

INDIVIDUAL OR SMALL GROUP

Make chalk or tape lines on the ground or the floor. Give each child a beanbag or koosh ball and assign him his own line. Have the child start at one end of his line and toss the beanbag or ball in front of himself, trying to make it land on the line or close to it. Tell the child to hop on one foot to retrieve the beanbag, and then hop back to the starting position. Repeat the process of throwing and hopping, but have him hop on the other foot the next time. As he becomes comfortable with his hopping skills, encourage him to throw the beanbag farther.

# Hop-a-Shape

DEVELOPING

INDIVIDUAL OR SMALL GROUP

Create a variety of large shapes on the ground with chalk or on the floor with tape. Make squares, ovals, rectangles, figure eights, or anything else you wish. The shapes should be large enough so the children can hop around their perimeters. Starting each child at a different shape, have her stand on her right foot and then hop around the outside of the shape. Tell her move to another shape, change to her left foot, and repeat the activity. Continue moving children to different shapes for as long as their stamina or success rate allows. Remind them to change the foot they are hopping on each time they move to another shape.

# Hopping All the Way

DEVELOPING

INDIVIDUAL, SMALL GROUP,
OR WHOLE GROUP

Create a traditional hopscotch pattern on a carpet runner with tape or paint, or outside with chalk. Give each child a koosh ball or beanbag. Model for them how to throw it and then retrieve it by hopping on one foot. If they are unable to do this, support them as they hop on one foot to get the ball, and then have them hop on both feet on the way back until they become stronger and more confident. If you wish, add letters, numbers, or words to each hopscotch square and ask children to read them as they retrieve their beanbags or balls. If you are doing this activity with your whole group, make several hopscotch patterns, divide children into groups of three or four, and monitor their hopping.

# "Hopstacle" Course

INDIVIDUAL

DEVELOPING/PROFICIENT

In a gymnasium, hallway, or outside, create an obstacle course for the child to hop her way through. You might make a wavy tape line to hop alongside, include hula hoops or cones to hop around, plastic stepping spots to hop on, and small objects to hop over. Be sure to remind her that after each obstacle, she should switch feet so that both legs are getting hopping practice. Consider allowing her to set up and travel through a course she has designed.

# Skill: Balances on one foot with eyes open.

When a child is first learning to balance, be sure to provide support as needed. Once the child becomes more secure in her ability, reduce the amount of support but remember to keep her success rate high. The goal is to get the child to be able to balance on one leg for at least six seconds at a time. (Most children start at one or two seconds in their early attempts.) For those children who seem to struggle even in the beginning stages of balancing, continue to work on running, jumping, hopping, and balance board activities.

## Paired Support                                              BEGINNING

**INDIVIDUAL, SMALL GROUP (in pairs),
OR WHOLE GROUP (in pairs)**

This activity requires pairs, so if you have an odd number of children or just one child, pair up with the child by sitting in a chair while he stands. Bring them to a space where they have enough room to extend their legs to each side. Have partners face each other and put the palms of their hands against those of their partner, extending their arms in front of themselves as far as possible. When each pair is in position, begin giving directions, such as "left knee up." Each child brings his left knee up in front of him for a moment and then back down to the standing position. The goal is to give children a sense of standing on one leg but with the security of someone to counterbalance their weight until they master the skill.

## Baby Steps                                                  BEGINNING

**INDIVIDUAL OR SMALL GROUP (in pairs)**

Place a low box on the floor of your work area or bring the child to a set of stairs. Have her keep one foot on the floor and place the other on the box or first stair. Tell the child to alternate placing her foot on the object and then back on the floor. Repeat with the other foot. Once she has her balance in the "on" position, ask her to lift her foot off the object for a second or two, and then place her foot back on it. Increase the length of time her foot is in the air as she becomes better able to balance on one leg.

# Simon Keeps on Saying

BEGINNING

INDIVIDUAL, SMALL GROUP,
OR WHOLE GROUP

This activity builds children's ability to balance with confidence. Gather them in an open space that's free of obstacles and provides each child with adequate room. Ask the children to do specific actions, but precede each request with "Simon says." For example, you might say, "Simon says stand with your feet together and arms out at your sides." "Simon says stand on your right foot, lift your left foot, and put your hands on your hips." "Simon says stand on your toes with your arms out and then put your hands on your hips." "Simon says lift your right foot and swing it back and forth." As the children become more confident, decrease the two-legged activities and increase the one-legged activities.

# One-Legged Statues

BEGINNING

INDIVIDUAL, SMALL GROUP,
OR WHOLE GROUP

Bring the children to an open space like a gymnasium or to a field outside. Model how you want them to move around the space (walk, shuffle, dance, sidestep, etc.) and what to do when you say "Statues!" (Freeze in any position they want as long as they are balancing on one leg only.) Start out by telling them to walk around, and after a few seconds say "Statues!" At first, allow just a second or two for "freeze" time, but gradually increase it as the children become more skilled.

GROSS MOTOR SKILLS

# Frankenstein

BEGINNING

INDIVIDUAL, SMALL GROUP, OR WHOLE GROUP

This one is simple and fast. Bring the children to an open area and model how to walk like Frankenstein does in the movies, arms straight out in front and legs straight and stiff. Hold one leg up for an exaggerated period of time before taking a step and then do the same with your other leg. Have the children mimic your actions and move around the space freely, keeping each leg up for as long as they can before switching.

# Tap by Color

BEGINNING/DEVELOPING

INDIVIDUAL OR SMALL GROUP

Place three different colored plastic stepping spots on the floor in your work area. Space them fairly close together in one row of three. Have the child stand facing the spots; then name a color for her and specify right or left foot. Tell her to locate that color spot and tap it three times with the foot you indicated. So if you said "Blue, left," she would tap the blue spot with her left foot three times. (If a child is unable to tap three times without losing her balance, decrease the number.) As she becomes more secure, add a second row of colored spots above the original three. As before, name the color and the foot you want her to use. If you are working with several children, give each one a set of plastic stepping spots. If desired, write words, letters, numbers, or shapes on the stepping spots and direct the child by what's written on each spot.

# No-Hands Hokey Pokey

INDIVIDUAL, SMALL GROUP, OR WHOLE GROUP

DEVELOPING

Place a hula hoop on the ground outside or on the floor of your work space (or make a hoop out of string, rope, or tape). Have the children stand around it. If you are working with only one child, join her somewhere on the outside of the hoop. This activity is similar to the traditional version of the Hokey Pokey except that you will be using only the legs, knees, toes, and heels rather than the whole body. The goal is to have the children balancing on one leg as often as possible, for a few seconds each time. Sing the song and have the children join in for the chorus.

# Balancing Act

INDIVIDUAL, SMALL GROUP, OR WHOLE GROUP

DEVELOPING

Give the children beanbags and have them place them on their heads. Allow some time for them to get comfortable keeping the beanbags in place while standing on two feet. Then challenge them to keep the beanbags on their heads while balancing on one leg. If their beanbag falls off, have them put it back on their head and see if they can balance one second longer before it falls off again. If they're really up for a challenge, see if they can switch the leg they are balancing on while keeping the beanbag in place.

# Skill: Balances on one foot with eyes closed (6 or more seconds).

Balancing with eyes closed is significantly more difficult than with eyes open because it removes the visual cues we use to support our body position. Be sure to keep safety in mind when doing the activities that follow. Also make certain that the child is comfortable balancing with her eyes open before you ask her to do so with her eyes closed. Many of the activities with the previous skill ("Balances on one foot with eyes open," pages 132–135) can be adapted for this next skill.

## Letting Go                                               BEGINNING
**INDIVIDUAL OR SMALL GROUP**

Have the child stand next to a table, chair, chalk ledge, or something else that's sturdy and of similar height. Ask him to hold onto it with one hand and close his eyes. Then tell him to lift his left foot off the ground and hold it for a few seconds before placing it back on the floor. Count the seconds for him if you wish. Have him do the same thing with his right foot, again with his eyes closed. Continue to alternate between the two feet, gradually extending the amount of time the child is on just one foot. Next, tell him to let go of what he was holding onto and to take one small step away and repeat the activity.

## One, Then Two, Then Three                               BEGINNING
**INDIVIDUAL**

Ask the child to face you, hold your hands, and close her eyes. From this position, you will be able to steady her if necessary. Tell her to lift one foot off the ground for a count of one, and then do the same with the other foot. If she is successful with a count of one, encourage her to repeat the activity but to hold each foot up for a count of two, and then three. Be sure not to push the child further than she is ready to go. Keeping steady and being successful for a count of two or three is good progress toward the final goal.

# Marching in the Dark

BEGINNING/DEVELOPING

INDIVIDUAL, SMALL GROUP,
OR WHOLE GROUP

Make sure the children can march in place with eyes open before doing this task with eyes closed. Then have each child stand up, close his eyes, and march in place. Gradually increase the marching time. Once the child can march comfortably with his eyes shut for 10 seconds, have him try marching with a cross-lateral motion, touching one hand to the opposite knee.

# Open Them, Shut Them

DEVELOPING/PROFICIENT

INDIVIDUAL, SMALL GROUP,
OR WHOLE GROUP

Stand facing the children. Ask them to copy the one-legged poses you show them with their eyes open. As the children mimic each one correctly, have them do the same poses again, but with their eyes closed. Encourage them to hold each pose for as long as they can and celebrate every attempt.

# Steady as You Go

DEVELOPING/PROFICIENT

INDIVIDUAL OR SMALL GROUP

Have the child stand facing you. Tell her to shut her eyes and lift one foot off the ground for a count of two. Celebrate her success, and then have her do the same with the other foot. If she is successful with a count of two, encourage her to repeat the activity while holding each foot up for a count of three, four, five, or six seconds. Be sure not to push the child further than she is ready to go. Steady balance will develop with practice.

# One-Leg Swing

INDIVIDUAL OR SMALL GROUP

DEVELOPING/PROFICIENT

Bring the child to an area large enough for him to straighten out either leg in any direction. When he's comfortable balancing on one leg with eyes open, start giving directions for him to swing his other leg forward, backward, or sideways. Call out each direction one or two times, have the child switch legs, and then repeat the directions in any order you choose. At first, the swinging motion can be subtle. As he becomes more skilled, encourage the child to make broader swings with each leg. Then tell him to close his eyes, balance on one leg, and follow your directions with the raised leg. If he loses balance while doing this, allow him to open his eyes, regain his stability, and continue but with his eyes shut again.

# **Skill:** Demonstrates standing cross-crawl (marching) pattern.

Cross crawl is simply an exaggeration of our normal walking movements. It is done by marching in place and raising the opposite arm and leg with each step: the right arm and the left leg move in tandem as do the left arm and the right leg. Children just learning this skill should begin by moving the legs only at first, and then incorporate the arm movements when they are ready. Music is particularly helpful in teaching children how to march in place, as it helps them keep a beat with their legs.

## Sitting Down on the Job

BEGINNING

INDIVIDUAL, SMALL GROUP, OR WHOLE GROUP

Have the children sit in chairs that allow their feet to touch the floor and their knees to be bent at right angles. Model how to raise the right knee and the left hand or the left knee and the right hand simultaneously while sitting, then ask them to try it. Start out slowly and give them verbal cues if needed. Once they become more secure with this movement, encourage them to tap the opposite knee with the hand. Play music to maintain a rhythmic pattern of movement.

# Opposites Attract

INDIVIDUAL

BEGINNING

Place a mat or blanket on the floor and have the child lie on his back with his knees bent. Take hold of one hand and the opposite knee (left hand and right knee), gently bring them together, and then return them to their original positions. Do this five times and then repeat with the opposing pair (right hand and left knee). Next, have the child make the movements without your help, coaching him with simple phrases, if necessary, such as "right hand to left knee." Once he is secure making the motion with each side separately, have him alternate both sides to mimic the traditional cross-crawl pattern while lying on his back. Practice this for 10 to 20 repetitions.

# Hula Hoop Hit

INDIVIDUAL, SMALL GROUP,
OR WHOLE GROUP

DEVELOPING

Give each child a small hula hoop. Show them how to hold it with their hands at hip height, with the rim of the hoop sticking out far enough in front of their bodies that their knees can hit the hoop easily. Model how to do the standing cross-crawl, making your knees hit the rim of the hoop each time you bring one up. Then ask the children to do the same thing with their hoops, first at their own pace, and then at a pace determined by you.

# How High Can You Go?

**INDIVIDUAL**

DEVELOPING

Ask the child to face you. (You may need to sit while the child stands for this activity, depending on her height.) Place your hands, palms down, in front of the child. Tell her to hit the palms of your hands with the tops of her knees in an alternating marching motion. You may need to start at a slow pace and give the child verbal cues to raise each knee. Hold your hands low at first and gradually raise them to an appropriate marching height as she becomes more skilled. Keep things interesting by asking the child to count numbers or say the alphabet as she marches.

# Mimic Me

**INDIVIDUAL OR SMALL GROUP**

DEVELOPING/PROFICIENT

Stand facing the child. Tell him to copy what you do, which will be the isolated movements in a cross-crawl motion. Raise your left leg with your knee bent and ask the child to do the same with his left leg. Lower your left leg, raise your right leg, and have the child do the same. Once the marching pattern is established, add cross-lateral hand movements. As your right knee reaches its highest point, touch it with your left hand. Then raise your left knee and touch it with your right hand. Begin slowly at first, and increase the pace gradually.

# Balloon Bop

**INDIVIDUAL, SMALL GROUP, OR WHOLE GROUP**

DEVELOPING/PROFICIENT

Bring the children to a hallway, gymnasium, or outside area. Give each one an inflated balloon and show them how to keep it in the air by bouncing it off their knees. Let them try it, using either knee at first until they get the hang of it. When their accuracy improves, require the children to hit the balloon with alternating knees only, staying in one spot as much as possible and mimicking a marching movement. (It might help to make an X on the floor or ground so the children have a visual reminder of where they should try to remain standing.)

# Cross-Crawl March in Place

PROFICIENT

INDIVIDUAL, SMALL GROUP,
OR WHOLE GROUP

Have the children stand and march in place, touching one hand to the opposite knee or thigh with each step. Start by marching at a normal pace, then vary the pace to slow or fast or back to normal, making sure every child is able to be successful. Practice this from 30 seconds to 2 minutes, integrating music, songs, or conversation while they march in place. Once they've mastered this, have them try cross-crawl marching while moving forward.

# Skill: Dribbles ball with one hand.

Before a child learns to dribble with one hand, she may actually need to start with two hands. Most of the activities that follow can be done with two hands, if that is what's appropriate for the child. Once she is dribbling with one hand, keep an eye out for patting, slapping, and floppy wrists, as these will inhibit the smooth motion of dribbling. The child's elbow and forearm should absorb the bounce and push the ball back down, and her eyes should be on the ball. In the early stages of developing this skill, use a lightweight ball that bounces easily. Move to a heavier one that requires more push as the child becomes more skilled.

## Got You Covered

INDIVIDUAL

BEGINNING

Stand behind the child and shadow her with the correct dribbling posture: feet about shoulder width apart, arms bent at waist height, and knees slightly flexed. Place your hand over her dominant hand and pretend to dribble an imaginary ball. When she's comfortable with the motion, introduce a ball and physically and verbally coach her in bouncing it.

## On My Cue

INDIVIDUAL

BEGINNING

Have the child show you the ready position for dribbling and correct any posture issues. Then kneel in front of the child and simulate a rising ball by holding a ball in the palm of your hand and raising it upward. Coach the child how to move his hand and arm up (as his finger pads are cushioning and receiving the rising ball) and then push down (as he continues the dribble). Move the ball faster and give fewer verbal cues as he becomes more independent. If he's ready, continue the cues but give him the ball to bounce on his own.

# Bouncin' to the Beat

BEGINNING/DEVELOPING

INDIVIDUAL, SMALL GROUP, OR WHOLE GROUP

Bring the children to a work space that is free of obstacles and give each one a playground ball. Play music that has a fairly regular beat and model how to dribble the ball to the same rhythm. Then give them a verbal signal each time they should be dribbling the ball. As they become more comfortable, eliminate the signal. Play faster music as their level of skill increases. Instead of playing music, you can also recite jump rope rhymes or clap a beat with your hands.

# Count and Bounce

BEGINNING/DEVELOPING

INDIVIDUAL OR SMALL GROUP

Write a number or make symbols representing a number on each of 6 to 10 plastic stepping spots. For example, one spot might have the numeral 3 written on it, another spot might have 6 dots drawn on it, and another 8 stars. Place them on the floor. Give the child a ball and tell her to walk from spot to spot and dribble the ball the number of times indicated on each spot. At first, arrange the spots in numerical order; later, place them in random order to provide practice with number value. If you're doing this with a small group, give each child his own ball and set of plastic stepping spots.

# Body Bounce

DEVELOPING

INDIVIDUAL, SMALL GROUP, OR WHOLE GROUP

Bring the children to a gymnasium or other space where they will have adequate room to practice. Give each child a vinyl ball (or playground ball). Tell them to start bouncing the balls with one hand at their own pace. Once they find their rhythm, start calling out specific tasks for them to attempt. For example, you might tell them to bounce their ball as high as their belly button, bounce it by their knees, or down around their ankles, and so on.

Number Facts & Jumping Jacks

# Inner Circle

**INDIVIDUAL OR SMALL GROUP**

DEVELOPING

It's important for a child to learn to bounce a ball at an appropriate distance from her body to keep it from hitting her feet. To reinforce this, place a hula hoop (or circle of string) on the floor in your work area and have each child stand inside the hoop with her toes about four inches from the edge. Tell the child to bounce the ball in front of her as many times as she can, making sure it stays outside the hoop each time. The same exercise can be done when the child is ready to bounce a ball to her side.

# Now You See It, Now You Don't

**INDIVIDUAL, SMALL GROUP, OR WHOLE GROUP**

DEVELOPING

Give each child a playground ball (or a ball of similar size) and an open space to work in. Have the children begin dribbling the balls. Every few seconds say "Look at me" or something similar. That's the signal for each child to look away from the ball for a moment while continuing to dribble it. As the children get better at controlling the ball, ask them to look at you more often and for longer periods of time.

# Walk the Line

**INDIVIDUAL OR SMALL GROUP**

DEVELOPING/PROFICIENT

Tape a wide, wavy, or zigzag line on the floor of your work space. Show the child how to dribble the ball on or close to the line while walking along it. Allow her to practice dribbling and traveling at her own speed. If a wavy line is too challenging, start with a straight line and move onto more challenging lines as her success rate increases. If you're working with more than one child, give each one her own line and ball.

# Copycat Bounce

**DEVELOPING/PROFICIENT**

INDIVIDUAL OR SMALL GROUP

Give each child a large playground ball and keep one for yourself. Tell the children to copy you as you do various dribbling actions. For example, you might dribble the ball a few times with your left hand and then your right hand; bounce it while moving sideways; dribble it as you skip, shuffle, or run; and dribble it high or low. In addition, explain to them that when you say "Hold it!" they are to stop dribbling the ball and hold it with both hands until you start dribbling yours again. If desired, you and the children can take turns being the leader, so you'll be copying a child's dribbling actions too.

# Skill: Dribbles ball with alternating hands.

Dribbling with alternating hands requires high-level integration of both sides of the brain. When a child can dribble well with one hand, challenge him to try alternating hands. At first, he'll want to look at the ball while he is dribbling; allow him to do so until he becomes more skilled. Encourage him to practice good dribbling posture and remind him to push the ball down (instead of slapping it), maintain relaxed fingers and arms so he'll be ready to receive the ball, and keep the ball in front of his body as he dribbles.

## Air Dribbling

BEGINNING

INDIVIDUAL, SMALL GROUP, OR WHOLE GROUP

Give each child an inflated balloon and enough room to move around freely. The balloon won't bounce, but this activity will give them practice using alternating hands in a dribbling rhythm while using a slow-moving object. Model how to tap the balloon underhand by hitting it up with one hand and then the other. Then have the children do the same, encouraging them to use alternating hands as often as possible. If desired, children can count how many times they were able to tap the balloon using a left-hand, right-hand pattern.

## One, Then the Other

BEGINNING

INDIVIDUAL, SMALL GROUP, OR WHOLE GROUP

Give each child a large playground ball and have him begin bouncing it with his preferred hand. After he has successfully completed 10 or 12 consecutive bounces, ask him to see how many times he can bounce it with his other hand. Have him continue practicing in this manner until he can use his nondominant hand for at least 6 smooth bounces.

# Dribble and Pause

**INDIVIDUAL OR SMALL GROUP**

BEGINNING

As children begin to use alternate hands for dribbling, they may need extra practice to learn to make this movement pattern fluid. Model for the children how to start dribbling with the left hand and then scoop the ball with the right hand, pausing briefly before releasing it. Then dribble with the right hand, scoop with the left hand, and pause briefly. Give each child a large playground ball and ask them to do the same dribble-scoop-pause pattern over and over.

# Lefty Righty

**INDIVIDUAL OR SMALL GROUP**

BEGINNING

Have each child start with a large playground ball in her right hand and bounce it close to her feet in front of herself. As the ball bounces back up, tell her to use her left hand to bounce it this time and then her right hand, and so forth. Have her repeat the pattern as long as she can, giving fewer verbal cues as her bouncing becomes more rhythmic.

# Crazy 8 Times 10

**INDIVIDUAL**

DEVELOPING

Create a large figure eight (at least 12 feet long) on the floor of your work space with tape or with chalk if you're working outside on a level surface. First have the child hold the ball while he walks the figure eight a couple of times to get accustomed to the path. Then have him dribble the ball with one hand while walking the figure eight. When he is successful with this, have him try alternate-hand dribbling, with a goal of walking through the pattern 10 times.

# Walk 'n Bounce                                    DEVELOPING
INDIVIDUAL OR SMALL GROUP

Give the child a large playground ball. Ask her to dribble the ball with alternate hands as she walks around a simple path, indoors or outdoors. Make sure the path is wide and easy to follow. As her skills develop, have her negotiate a more complex course.

# Look Away                                         DEVELOPING
INDIVIDUAL OR SMALL GROUP

Once children can dribble a ball with alternating hands, encourage them to look away from the ball as they bounce it. Stand facing the children and have them begin dribbling. Then have them look at you after every few bounces. As their skills increase, tell them to look at you for as long as they can before losing control of the ball.

# Long-Distance Dribble                             DEVELOPING/PROFICIENT
INDIVIDUAL OR SMALL GROUP

As their skills develop, provide a space that is large enough for the children to practice alternate-hand dribbling over a long distance. In a gymnasium, along a hallway, or around a track are good spaces for this activity. Keep it fun and work toward mastery of this skill.

# Grounded                                          DEVELOPING/PROFICIENT
INDIVIDUAL OR SMALL GROUP

As the children become more skilled, have them try dribbling the ball with alternating hands while kneeling. Tell them to start out with small gentle bounces, tapping the ball softly and keeping it close to the floor. Then have them increase the speed and height of each bounce. If a child is struggling with this, allow him to use just one hand for a few bounces, then the other hand for a few bounces. Once he's comfortable with that, have him try alternating hands again.

# Skill: Skips smoothly for at least 10 yards.

Skipping is one of the most difficult locomotion skills a child will learn. Children who have trouble skipping should be encouraged to master hopping, jumping, and single-leg balancing first, as those actions are the basis for the movements required to skip fluidly. When teaching children to skip, it is important to make sure that the action occurs on the balls of the feet, that the hop is low to the ground, and that the body leans slightly forward.

## Talking Through It

BEGINNING

INDIVIDUAL OR
SMALL GROUP

Talk the children through each step of the skipping process. Begin slowly until each has a sense of the rhythm with cues like "step right, hop, step left, hop." Skip next to the children during this first phase of learning, allowing them to see and hear the correct movements.

## Hop and Balance

BEGINNING

INDIVIDUAL OR
SMALL GROUP

Model this activity for the children first. Hop once, and then pause and balance on the same foot. Hop again, and then pause and balance on the other foot. Tell the children to hop, pause, and then balance on one foot for two seconds, then hop, pause, and balance on the other foot for two seconds. Vary the time allowed for balancing from two seconds to five seconds.

## Together We Go

INDIVIDUAL

BEGINNING

Bring the child to an open space like a gymnasium, hallway, or outside area. Model smooth skipping for him, giving verbal cues about what your body is doing while you skip. Then take the child's hand and have him skip with you, continuing to verbalize the steps as you go. Eventually, skip with the child without saying the steps. Align your pace with the child's skill level but encourage him to move a little faster when he is ready, as it is easier to skip when the pace is quickened.

## Skip to My Lou

INDIVIDUAL, SMALL GROUP, OR WHOLE GROUP

BEGINNING/DEVELOPING

Skipping to music is an easy way to help children incorporate rhythm into the movement and to skip smoothly. Play a song with a regular beat and ask the children to skip to that beat around your work space. Start with slightly slow music until skipping skills are more secure, and then speed it up. If you are working with a group of children, have them link elbows every now and then during the song and do a "Skip to My Lou" by skipping around in a circle once before releasing each other. If you have enough space, do this with your whole group.

## Turn, Turn, Turn

INDIVIDUAL, SMALL GROUP, OR WHOLE GROUP

DEVELOPING

Bring the children to an open field or gymnasium. Tell them that as they practice skipping, you will give them a signal (like blowing a whistle or calling out "Turn!") every few seconds, which means that they are to change the direction they are skipping in. Have them watch out for each other and skip instead of run. Continue for as long as their stamina allows.

# Skipping Around

**INDIVIDUAL OR SMALL GROUP**

DEVELOPING

Set up cones, boxes, plastic stepping spots, or chairs in random patterns around your work area. Space them far enough apart so that the children can easily skip around each one. Start with a few obstacles but increase the number as children become more skilled. If you are working with a small group, set up several separate courses, being sure each one provides adequate space. Tell the children to skip around each object once before moving onto the next course, and to move at a pace that is comfortable for them.

# Zigzag Path

**INDIVIDUAL OR SMALL GROUP**

DEVELOPING

Create two parallel, zigzag lines on the floor with tape, leaving a generous amount of space between them. Tell the child to skip from one end to the other, following the contours of the path and staying within the lines. Once she skips with ease three separate times, narrow the space between the lines and repeat the exercise. If you are doing this with a small group, make a zigzag path for each child or each pair of children.

# Skip, You're It!

**SMALL GROUP OR WHOLE GROUP**

DEVELOPING/PROFICIENT

Bring the children to the gymnasium or playground. Explain that they will be playing a traditional game of tag, but instead of running, they will be skipping. Determine which child will be "It" and then let the others start skipping before he begins. Once everyone is in motion, if a child gets tagged, he freezes until someone skips over and releases him. At that point he can start skipping again. Change the tagger as frequently as you wish.

# Skill: Demonstrates smooth jumping jacks.

Getting their arms and legs to work in unison is a challenge for some children, so you may need to break this skill into two parts. Once the child can do each action in isolation, then it's time to put the movements together. Ideally the child should jump on the balls of her feet and look straight ahead. You might consider having the children do jumping jacks while counting in any sequence or reciting the days of the week, the months of the year, or the alphabet. The rhythm of the words can help them maintain a jumping rhythm.

## Arms Up

BEGINNING

INDIVIDUAL, SMALL GROUP, OR WHOLE GROUP

Bring the children to an area where they can extend their arms fully without touching anything or anyone. Model how to do the arm movements only for jumping jacks. Begin with your arms down at your sides, then move them in synchrony to above your head, touch your hands together, and bring the arms back down at your sides. Tell the children to watch you do it, then do it with you, and finally do it on their own with verbal prompts from you.

## Get Your Feet Moving

BEGINNING

INDIVIDUAL, SMALL GROUP, OR WHOLE GROUP

Model how to perform the foot movements for jumping jacks. (For the purpose of this exercise, keep your hands on your hips.) Begin with your feet together. Jump slightly, moving the feet apart in synchrony and landing on separated feet. Jump again and bring the feet back together. Tell the children to watch you, do it with you, and then do it on their own with verbal cues from you.

# All Together Now

**BEGINNING**

INDIVIDUAL

Use a work space that offers enough room for you and the child to do jumping jacks safely. Stand in front of the child and model the movements: arms up and feet apart, then arms down and feet together. Tell her to join in and do a few with you. Start out slowly and increase the speed as she shows more fluid movements.

# Practice Makes Perfect

**DEVELOPING**

INDIVIDUAL OR
SMALL GROUP

Individually, in pairs, or in a small group, have the children practice jumping jacks. Set easy goals at first, such as doing three to five smooth, slow jumping jacks. As their skills improve, increase the number to 10, 20, or a jumping jack for each letter of the alphabet. Make sure the children are having fun and are successful with each round of practice.

# Jump to the Beat

**DEVELOPING**

INDIVIDUAL, SMALL GROUP, OR WHOLE GROUP

Have the children face you while you beat a rhythm on a drum or with wooden blocks. Tell them that with each beat, they are to do one half of a jumping jack. Gradually increase the beat until the children are doing full, smooth jumping jacks.

# Read and Jump

**DEVELOPING**

INDIVIDUAL

Write on a whiteboard, in a horizontal line, the letters, numbers, or words that the child knows independently. Have him read these as he practices jumping jacks, one word for each complete action. Challenge him to get through the entire list without stopping his jumping or his reading.

# Jumping Jack Chants

**INDIVIDUAL OR SMALL GROUP**

DEVELOPING

Gather a collection of jump rope rhymes you can read or recordings of rhymes you can play. "Teddy Bear, Teddy Bear" is a good example. Bring the children to an open space. Begin one of the rhymes and have the children do jumping jacks to its rhythm. If necessary, model this for each new chant.

# Close Your Eyes

**INDIVIDUAL**

DEVELOPING/PROFICIENT

Once a child is fairly skilled at jumping jacks, challenge her to do them with her eyes closed. Bring her to a space that is free of any obstacles and have her do one jumping jack with her eyes open, one with her eyes closed, then one with eyes open, and two with eyes closed. Continue increasing the number of jumping jacks she does with her eyes closed as her skill and comfort level dictate.

# Circle Jacks

**INDIVIDUAL OR SMALL GROUP**

DEVELOPING/PROFICIENT

Bring the child to a space that is large enough to do jumping jacks and turns without hitting anyone or anything. Model how to do jumping jacks while making quarter turns with your body during each jump, and then have the child try it. After four or more quarter turns, have her reverse direction and do four or more again.

GROSS MOTOR SKILLS

# References

Ayres, J., J. Robbins, and S. McAfee. 2005. *Sensory Integration and the Child: Understanding Hidden Sensory Challenges.* Los Angeles, CA: Western Psychological Services.

Berch, D. 2005. "Making sense of number sense." *Journal of Learning Disabilities*, 38(4): 333–339.

Clements, D. H. and J. Serama. 2009. *Learning and Teaching Early Math: The Learning Trajectories Approach.* New York: Routledge.

Corbin, C. B. and R. P. Pangrazi. 1992. "Are American children and youth fit?" *Research Quarterly for Exercise & Sport*, 63(2): 96–106.

Greene, L. and M. Adeyanju. 1991. "Exercise and fitness guidelines for elementary and middle school children." *Elementary School Journal*, 91(5): 437–444.

Griffin, S. 2004. "Teaching number sense." *Educational Leadership*, 61(5): 39.

Halberda, J., M. Mazzocco, and L. Feigenson. 2008. "Individual differences in nonverbal number acuity correlate with maths achievement." *Nature*, 455: 665–668.

Hannaford, C. 2005. *Smart Moves: Why Learning Is Not All in Your Head.* Salt Lake City, UT: Great River Books.

Kranowitz, C. 2005. *The Out-of-Sync Child: Recognizing and Coping with Sensory Processing Disorder.* New York: Perigee.

Kuntzleman, C. T. 1993. "Childhood fitness: What is happening? What needs to be done?" *Preventive Medicine*, 22(4): 520–532.

Lembke, E., A. Foegen, T. Whittaker, and D. Hampton. 2008. "Establishing technically adequate measures of progress in early numeracy." *Assessment for Effective Intervention*, 33(4): 206–214.

Liddle, T. L. and L. Yorke. 2003. *Why Motor Skills Matter.* New York: McGraw-Hill.

Lillard, A. S. 2005. *Montessori: The Science Behind the Genius.* Oxford, NY: Oxford University Press, Inc.

Locuniak, M. and N. Jordan. 2008. "Using kindergarten number sense to predict calculation fluency in second grade." *Journal of Learning Disabilities*, 41(5): 451–459.

Louv, R. 2005. *Last Child in the Woods.* Chapel Hill, NC: Algonquin Books.

McGinnis, J. M., ed. 1987. "Summary of Findings from National Children and Youth Fitness Study II." *Journal of Physical Education, Recreation & Dance*, 56(1): 44–90.

Pass, S. 2004. *Parallel Paths to Constructivism: Jean Piaget and Lev Vygotsky.* Charlotte, NC: Information Age Publishing.

Pica, R. 2004. *Experiences in Movement: Birth to Age Eight.* Clifton Park, NY: Delmar.

Ratey, J. 2008. *Spark: The Revolutionary New Science of Exercise and the Brain.* New York: Little Brown.

# Index

**Note:** Page numbers in *italics* indicate Reproducibles.

### A

Activities, how to choose, 6. *See also activities listed under specific skills*

Adding on or taking away from a group (to 10), 63; activities for practicing: Back and Forth, 65; Counting Cookies, 64; Eraser Race, 64; Little Bo Peep, 63; Sticky Note Parade, 63; Traffic Jam, 64

Adding on or taking away from a group (to 100), 72; activities for practicing: Abacus Antics, 74; Color Me, 72; Flipping Out, 73; Number Spies, 73; Roll of the Dice, 73; Round and Round We Go, 72; Where Are You?, 74

Assessment of Gross Motor Skills, 6, *89–90*

Assessment of Numeracy Skills, 6, *14–16*

### B

Balancing on one foot with eyes closed (6 or more seconds), 136; activities for practicing: Letting Go, 136; Marching in the Dark, 137; One, Then Two, Then Three, 136; One-Leg Swing, 138; Open Them, Shut Them, 137; Steady as You Go, 137

Balancing on one foot with eyes open, 132; activities for practicing: Baby Steps, 132; Balancing Act, 135; Frankenstein, 134; No-Hands Hokey Pokey, 135; One-Legged Statues, 133; Paired Support, 132; Simon Keeps on Saying, 133; Tap by Color, 134

Beginning skill level, 5, 6, 7

Building/drawing objects reflecting an understanding of relative size, 32; activities for practicing: Big, Bigger, Biggest, 32; Under Construction I, 33; Under Construction II, 34; Do You See What I See?, 34; House Is a House, A, 32; Me in the Middle, 33; In Real Life, 35; Same Size Scavenger Hunt, 34

### C

Challenges facing teachers, 6

Combining objects to make a greater number, 47; activities for practicing: Counting Frame Combos, 49; Cube Connections, 48; Fast Fingers, 49; Follow the Recipe, 48; Jingle Bells in a Jar, 48; Joker's Wild, 49; Target Totals, 47

Counting objects aloud with accuracy (to 10), 22; Counting in Your Mind, 24; Graph About You, A, 23; I Spy, 23; One to Ten, 22; Pile It On, 24; Roll and Count, 22; Show Me the Money, 24; Ten Apples, 23

Counting objects aloud with accuracy (to 100), 50; activities for practicing: Bagging Groceries, 50; Birds on a Wire, 52; Eggs in a Basket, 51; Grab Bag, 51; Magic Wand, 50; Pennies in the Piggy, 51; You Can Count on It, 52

Counting steps aloud with accuracy (to 10), 18; activities for practicing: Down the Garden Path, 18; Every Which Way, 21; Follow My Lead, 19; Guided Tour, 18; Number Ladders, 21; By the Numbers, 20; From Place to Place, 20; In Step, 20; Step-Scotch, 19; Throw and Go, 19

Creating patterns when building or drawing, 40; activities for practicing: Crazy Caterpillars, 41; Edible Patterns, 42; Egg-cellent Patterns, 41; High-Tech Patterns, 43; I've Been Working on the Railroad, 42; Main Street, 43; Pattern Chains, 40; Patterned Parking, 40; Pocket Patterns, 43; Snazzy Snakes, 42; Socks in a Row, 41

### D

Demonstrating catching skills with large ball, 113; activities for practicing: Ball Bonanza, 114; Balloons for Beginners, 114; Bouncing Around, 115; Buddy Ball, 115; Catching in Circles, 116; Coming Up Short, 116; Old Softy, 113; Roll with It, 113; Throw It to Yourself, 114; Wall Ball, 116

Demonstrating catching skills with small ball or beanbag, 117; activities for practicing: Bouncing Baby Ball, 118; Crazy Catcher, 119; Got Milk?, 118; Juggler, The, 117; Partner Wall Ball, 119; So Big, 117; Toss and Touch, 118; Triple Play or Four Square, 119

Demonstrating smooth jumping jacks, 153; activities for practicing: All Together Now, 154; Arms Up, 153; Circle Jacks, 155; Close Your Eyes, 155; Get Your Feet Moving, 153; Jumping Jack Chants, 155; Jump to the Beat, 154; Practice Makes Perfect, 154; Read and Jump, 154

Demonstrating standing cross-crawl (marching) pattern, 139; activities for practicing: Balloon Bop, 141; Cross-Crawl March in Place, 142; How High Can You Go?, 141; Hula Hoop Hit, 140; Mimic Me, 141; Opposites Attract, 140; Sitting Down on the Job, 139

Demonstrating underhand throwing skills, 110; activities for practicing: Bowling for Bottles, 111; Hand to Hand, 111; Hole in One, 112; Partner Pass, 110; Pretend for Practice, 110; Scarf Juggling, 112; Wad It Up, 111

Developing skill level, 5, 6, 7

Developmental skills profiles, 6, 7; Gross Motor Skills Profile, 6, 7, *86*; Numeracy Skills Profile, 5, 7, *10*

Dribbling ball with alternating hands, 147; activities for practicing: Air Dribbling, 147; Crazy 8 Times 10, 148; Dribble and Pause, 148; Grounded, 149; Lefty Righty, 148; Long-Distance Dribble, 149; Look Away, 149; One, Then the Other, 147; Walk 'n Bounce, 149

Dribbling ball with one hand, 143; activities for practicing: Body Bounce, 144; Bouncin' to the Beat, 144; Copycat Bounce, 146; Count and Bounce, 144; Got You Covered, 143; Inner Circle, 145; On My Cue, 143; Now You See It, Now You Don't, 145; Walk the Line, 145

**E**

Estimating distance (by taking steps, using blocks, etc.), 44; activities for practicing: Babies and Giants, 45; Block by Block, 44; Guess and Step, 46; Measure and Compare, 44; Miles to Go, 45; Taking a Tour, 45; Throw and Guess, 46

**G**

Gross motor skills: balances on one foot with eyes closed (6 or more seconds), 136–38; balances on one foot with eyes open, 132–35; de-emphasis on, 6; deficiency of, 5; demonstrates catching skills with large ball, 113–16; demonstrates catching skills with small ball or beanbag, 117–19; demonstrates smooth jumping jacks, 153–55; demonstrates standing cross-crawl (marching) pattern, 139–42; demonstrates underhand throwing skills, 110–12; dribbles ball with alternating hands, 147–49; dribbles ball with one hand, 143–46; hops on alternating feet, 128–31; hops two-legged, 124–27; importance of, 5; jumps on mini-tramp, 106–9; pace for learning, 7; procedures for assessment of, 6, *89–90*; purpose of building, 91; runs well on flat ground, 96–99; runs well on uneven surfaces, 100–101; skips smoothly for at least 10 yards, 150–52; stands with confidence on balance board, 102–5; walks on balance beam or line, 120–23; walks with balance and spatial awareness, 92–95

Gross Motor Skills Profile, 6, 7, *86*

Gross Motor Skills Rubric, *87–88*

**H**

Hopping on alternating feet, 128; activities for practicing: Hop-a-Line, 130; Hop-a-Shape, 130; Hopping All the Way, 130; "Hopstacle" Course, 131; Hop with Me, 128; Number Jumping, 129; One Foot, Two Feet, 129; Stay Put, 128

Hopping two-legged, 124; activities for practicing: Climbing the Ladder, 125; Hop, Of Course!, 127; Hop Along, 125; Hop and Kick, 126; Hop and Seek, 126; Hop in Place Plus, 124; Hopping Hollywood Squares, 126; Hoppin' to the Rhythm, 124; Mix It Up, 125

**I**

Identifying place values (ones, tens, hundreds, thousands), 75; activities for practicing: Colorful Place Value, 78; Face Up Match, 76; Highlighters, 77; High Roller, 76; Mystery Numbers, 77; Popsicle Stick Place Value, 75; Rollin' to 100, 75; Show Me a Number, 77; Where Are You Now?, 76

**J**

Jumping on mini-tramp, 106; activities for practicing: Clapping All the Way, 108; Forward & Backward, 108; Jumping in a Circle, 109; Jumping Jack Jam, 108; Left Leg, Right Leg, 109; Mini-Tramp March, 107;

Jumping on mini-tramp (*continued*)
Now You've Got It, 106; Starting Out, 106; Throw and Catch, 109; Tippy Toes, 107; Walking on the Moon, 107

**M**

Mathematics, building foundation for, 5

Modeling basic fine motor patterns, 29; activities for practicing: Fine Motor Charades, 31; Follow My Fingers, 30; Nap, Tap, Lap, and Clap, 31; Raggedy Wrists, 29; Rock, Paper, Scissors, 31; Tappers, 30; Trumpet Playing, 29; Twofer, 30

Modeling gross motor patterns, 25; activities for practicing: Animals in Action, 27; Follow the Leader, 28; Going Through Hoops, 26; Gross Motor Pattern Play, 28; One at a Time, 25; One Foot in Front of the Other, 25; One Side Then Two, 26; Opposites, 27; Patty-Cake in Parts, 26; Triple Play, 28; Two Back at You, 27

**N**

*Number Facts & Jumping Jacks:* for developing numeracy skills, 5; goals of, 4, 7; organization of, 6

Numeracy: components of, 4; using *Number Facts & Jumping Jacks* for developing, 5

Numeracy skills: adds on or takes away from a group (to 10), 63–65; adds on or takes away from a group (to 100), 72–74; benefits and importance of, 4, 17; builds/draws objects reflecting an understanding of relative size, 32–35; combines objects to make a greater number, 47–49; counts objects aloud with accuracy (to 10), 22–24; counts objects aloud with accuracy (to 100), 50–52; counts steps aloud with accuracy (to 10), 18–21; creates patterns when building or drawing, 40–43; estimates distance (by taking steps, using blocks, etc.), 44–46; identifies place values (ones, tens, hundreds, thousands), 75–78; models basic fine motor patterns, 29–31; models gross motor patterns, 25–28; pace for learning, 7; procedures for assessment of, 6, *14–16*; recognizes number groups to 10 without counting every object, 56–59; recognizes number groups to 100 without counting every object, 66–68; replicates patterns when building or drawing, 36–39; shows groups of objects by number (to 100), 69–71; shows groups of objects to correctly represent numbers to 10, 60–62; skip counts with manipulatives to a multiple of 10, 79–81; solves basic math problems with manipulatives, then transfers problems to paper, 82–84; understands concepts of add on and take away (using manipulatives), 53–55

Numeracy Skills Profile, 5, 7, *10*

Numeracy Skills Rubric, *11–13*

**P**

Physical activity, decline in, 5

Proficient skill level, 5, 6, 7

Procedures for Assessment of Gross Motor Skills, 6, *89–90*

Procedures for Assessment of Numeracy Skills, 6, *14–16*

**R**

Recognizing number groups to 10 without counting every object, 56; activities for practicing: Abacus Counting, 59; Finger Flash, 56; Lily Pads, 58; Lots of Dots, 57; Now You See Them, 58; Peek-a-Boo, 58; Spin a High Five, 57; Start Out Slowly, 56; Swatting Flies, 57

Recognizing number groups to 100 without counting every object, 66; activities for practicing: Base 10 Rides Again, 67; Count in a Flash, 68; Counting with Cubes, 67; Cut-Ups, 66; At the Movies, 67; Rainbow Rows, 66

Replicating patterns when building or drawing, 36; activities for practicing: Clippers, 39; Hide-and-Seek, 37; Just Hangin' Around, 37; Pattern Block Parade, 37; Pattern Pathways, 38; Patterns All Around, 36; Stackables, 39; Stamping Sequences, 38; Stick Patterns, 36; Towers of Patterns, 38

Response to Intervention initiative, 7

Responsive Instruction initiative, 7

Rubrics, 6, 7; Gross Motor Skills Rubric, *87–88*; Numeracy Skills Rubric, *11–13*

Running well on flat ground, 96; activities for practicing: Copycat, 98; Hold That Pose, 97; Keep the Beat, 96; Knee Highs, 98; Make a Face, Run in Place, 96; Obstacle Course Relay, 99; Simon Says, 98; Walk 'n Run, 97

Running well on uneven surfaces, 100; activities for practicing: Infinity Run, 101; Near and Far, 100; This Way and That Way, 101; Touch and Run, 100; Tricky Trail, 101

**S**

Showing groups of objects by number (to 100), 69; activities for practicing: Abacus Patterns, 70; Absolutely Abacus II, 69; Absolutely Abacus III, 71; Blocks and Cards, 70; Count and Connect I, 69; Count and Connect II, 71; Framed, 70

Showing groups of objects to correctly represent numbers to 10, 60; activities for practicing: Absolutely Abacus I, 62; Bowling for Numbers, 61; Dealer's Choice, 61; Draw and Draw, 60; Fast Figuring, 62; Inside Out, 61; Pickup Sticks, 60

Skip counting with manipulatives to a multiple of 10, 79; activities for practicing: Colorful Counting, 81; Connect and Count, 79; Count It Out, 80; Flash Card Abacus, 81; It's All in the Beads, 80; Picture Counting, 80; Show of Hands, A, 79

Skipping smoothly for at least 10 yards, 150; activities for practicing: Hop and Balance, 150; Skip, You're It!, 152; Skipping Around, 152; Skip to My Lou, 151; Talking Through It, 150; Together We Go, 151; Turn, Turn, Turn, 151; Zigzag Path, 152

Solving basic math problems with manipulatives, then transferring the problems to paper, 82; activities for practicing: On the Abacus, 83; Add 'em Up or Take 'em Away, 82; Cubes, 83; Let the Chips Fall, 82; Pay Day, 84; Squared, 83; Work Sheets, 84

Standing with confidence on balance board, 102; activities for practicing: Add-a-Bounce, 104; Balance, Catch, and Count, 104; Balance and Catch, 103; Getting Creative, 105; Getting Started, 102; Moving On, 103; From One Hand to the Other, 103; Table Games, 105; Target Practice, 104; Up, Up, and Away, 105

**T**

Teachers, challenges faced by, 6

Tiered instruction, 5

**U**

Understanding concepts of add on and take away (using manipulatives), 53; activities for practicing: Aba-Count, 55; Cube-It, 54; Laundry Day, 54; More and Less, 53; Pigs in the Puddle, 53; Stringing Beads, 55; From Zero to Six(ty), 55

**W**

Walking on balance beam or line, 120; activities for practicing: Alligator Alley, 121; Along the Line, 120; Crossover Balance Line, 123; Look at Me, 122; Mother May I?, 122; Stay on Track, 121; From Thick to Thin, 120; Variations on a Beam, 122

Walking with balance and spatial awareness, 92; activities for practicing: Crossover Walking, 95; Heads Up, 94; Human Checkers, 92; Locomotion, 95; Pass It On, 93; Rollin', Rollin', Rollin', 95; Speedsters, 94; At a Standstill, 93; Turn and Freeze, 94; Two-Step, The, 92

# Meeting the Standards

Here are some of the educational standards addressed by *Number Facts & Jumping Jacks:*

## MATHEMATICS

- Understands the meaning of numbers, relationships among numbers, and different ways of representing numbers (PreK–3).
- Demonstrates an ability to compute fluently (PreK–3).
- Estimates to a reasonable degree of accuracy (PreK–3).
- Recognizes patterns (PreK–3).
- Uses mathematical models to represent the addition and subtraction of whole numbers (PreK–3).
- Recognizes the names of numbers (K).
- Counts in sequence (K).
- Counts to identify a total number of objects (K).
- Recognizes the concept of addition as putting together and the concept of subtraction as taking apart (K).
- Recognizes, creates, analyzes, and makes comparisons among shapes (K).
- Understands place value (1).
- Extends a counting sequence (1).
- Uses addition and subtraction functions to solve problems (1 and 2).
- Incorporates an understanding of place value in performing addition and subtraction operations (2).
- Demonstrates ability to use multiplication and division to solve problems involving numbers up to 100 (3).

## PHYSICAL EDUCATION

- Understands movement strategies and tactics used to learn and perform physical activities (PreK–3).
- Demonstrates coordination in movement of small muscles (PreK–3).
- Demonstrates eye-hand coordination (PreK–3).
- Shows spatial awareness in performing gross motor activities (PreK–3).
- Shows an ability to engage safely in physical activity at an appropriately challenging level for a long enough period to increase heart rate and muscular strength (K–3).